BASIN of GOLD

Life in Boise Basin, 1862-1890

Arthur A. Hart,

ARTHUR A. HART

Idaho City Historical Foundation / Historic Idaho

IDAHO CITY HISTORICAL FOUNDATION, INCORPORATED
HISTORIC IDAHO, INCORPORATED
1986
Third Printing, 1993

The Idaho City Historical Foundation, Incorporated, is a non-profit
organization dedicated to the preservation and dissemination of the history
of Boise Basin. Historic Idaho, Incorporated, is similarly organized to
prepare and publish works on the history, architecture, and culture of
Idaho, and vicinity. Proceeds from the sale of this book will be used to
publish future titles in the series.

Printed by Lithocraft, Incorporated.

Typesetting by Campbell Communications

Photographs are from the collections of the Idaho State Historical Society
and the Idaho City Historical Foundation

Library of Congress Catalog Card Number 86-82758

TABLE OF CONTENTS

Foreword 5

Discovery 6

The People 10

Getting There 14

The Railroad Era 20

Celestials 22

Blacks in Boise Basin 29

Mining 30

Rites of Passage 36

Christmas 38

New Year's 39

Independence Day 42

Thanksgiving 46

Other Celebrations 47

Cockpits and Dog Fights . . . 52

Soiled Doves 53

Germans 56

Hurdy-Gurdy Girls 57

Johnny Kelly 58

Bands 61

Charles Ostner 63

Fire! Fire! 64

Bogus Gold 68

George Ainslie 70

Churches 73

Pinkham-Patterson 74

Pistols and Politics 76

Afterword 80

Acknowledgements 83

Cover: *Idaho City in 1865 from a lithograph published in San Francisco*

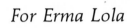

For Erma Lola

Forword

Boise Basin, in southwestern Idaho, is an area roughly 20 miles square, drained by dozens of small streams that run into Grimes and More creeks. They, in turn, run into Boise river. The entire basin is made up of hills and ridges that range in elevation from 3000 to 5000 feet, covered with pine and fir forests. Higher mountain ridges around the edges give the area its basin character.

This book attempts to capture the flavor of life in the bustling mining camps that grew up in a few short months after gold was discovered on Grimes creek in August, 1862. It is an account of people and events that reveal what it was like to live in Boise Basin in the years between 1862 and 1890 when Idaho became a state. In a work of this size it has not been possible, of course, to write anything like a complete history of the Basin, or to include more than a selection of the many stories that could be told about life in that group of small towns as they passed from booming gold rush camps into small but stable mining communities.

We have relied heavily upon eye-witness descriptions of people and events, and have allowed those who lived in Boise Basin at the time to tell what happened in their own words. Often biased or emotional, these accounts nevertheless have the merit of revealing attitudes and prejudices. People's perceptions of the truth usually influence their actions more than what is true. The words of those who lived in the Basin in the 19th Century have other qualities that make them worth quoting — they are often picturesque, witty, charming, and humorous. They have a spontaneity and immediacy rarely found in the later writing of scholars.

Welcome, then, to Idaho's Basin of Gold. I hope it is as much fun to read as it was to write.

Arthur A. Hart
Boise, 1986

Discovery

Following the discovery of gold in North Idaho in 1860 a steady stream of prospectors and miners poured into what was then the eastern part of Washington Territory. They fanned out across the rugged granite terrain of the Clearwater, Salmon river, Owyhee and other mountains, looking for prospects rich enough to justify staking claims and beginning full-scale mining. Prospectors looked for free gold in stream beds or gravel bars — particles that could be washed out by placering — or surface indications of gold-bearing quartz veins that could be worked by driving tunnels or shafts into the mountainside.

The discovery of Boise Basin's riches came on August 2, 1862, when a party of prospectors from Florence and Auburn, Oregon, found gold on Boston Bar near later Centerville. Although commonly called the Grimes party, the initial discovery group was really composed of three prospecting parties that had joined forces to explore the Basin in the summer of 1862. Moses Splawn, who had mined at Florence and Elk City, was the leader of one band, D. H. Fogus led another, and George Grimes a third. They got together in the Owyhee country, crossed a flooding Snake River with some difficulty, and struck out for Boise Basin. Fearing attack by the numerous Shoshoni Indians who lived in Boise Valley, they proceeded cautiously up the river to Boise canyon, then followed a northern ridge that led them into the Basin.

Moses Splawn's interest in the area had been aroused by a Bannock Indian, who uncharacteristically took the white man's mania for gold seriously enough to suggest that if the yellow metal was that important they could find it in abundance in Boise Basin.

On August 9, 1862, a week after D. H. Fogus found gold on Boston Bar, George Grimes was shot from ambush and killed. As Merle Wells points out, "Although a strong tradition persists in Boise Basin that the Indians had nothing to do with the shooting, those who returned to Walla Walla credited the incident to a disaffected Bannock or Shoshoni. In any event, Grimes was hastily buried in a prospect hole and his men hurried back to the Boise River . . ." (Grimes Creek and Grimes Pass were later named in honor of the unfortunate prospector and a monument erected at the spot where he was buried.)

1.
George Grimes' grave was pictured in this 1884 lithograph. One of Ben Willson's flumes runs past it.

2.
Prospectors explored the Basin with pack strings like this later one at Centerville.

3.
Pioneer City was usually called Hog'em by old-timers. It also went by the names Pioneerville or just plain Pioneer.

Pioneer City (first called Hog'em) and Idaho City (first called Bannock City or West Bannock) were started in October, 1862, after enlarged and well-supplied parties returned from Walla Walla. Reports that some placer claims were yielding as much as $200 per day per man reached Lewiston, Walla Walla, and Portland, leading to a mad rush to Boise Basin, even though the country was remote, trails virtually undeveloped, and roads for wheeled vehicles non-existent. A more serious difficulty was the fact that winter was coming on. Water for placering would not be available when streams froze and deep snows would make life miserable, if not actually dangerous.

Despite all that, they came — by the thousands. A contemporary, writing in Boise's *Capital Chronicle* a few years later, explained it: "They were, for the most part, veteran prospectors for gold. Many years of adventurous experiences all over the gold fields of California, Fraser river, Cariboo, Washington Territory and Eastern Oregon, had acquainted them with the general features and climatic changes of the entire gold producing region from British Columbia to Southern California. They were at home wherever they went — self-reliant and energetic to a remarkable degree. Hardships and privations had no terror; and peril, with a spice of adventure, had a positive charm for them."

Not all who joined the rush to Boise Basin late in 1862 quite fit this romantic description. As in every gold rush, there were men inadequately prepared, either physically or mentally, to endure the hardships. Some came without the supplies or the money they would need to last through a mountain winter. Many who hoped to find work to earn their keep were disappointed. The even larger population attracted to Idaho in the spring of 1863 included sober and industrious men who knew what they were doing, scoundrels and adventurers who came to prey on others, and large numbers of men without the skills or the capital to stick it out. Small wonder, then, that the Basin's spectacular inrush of people in 1863 and 1864 was followed by a period of stabilization when most of the disappointed fortune hunters drifted away to other excitements or went back to their former homes.

On March 4, 1863, President Abraham Lincoln signed legislation establishing Idaho Territory out of what had been the eastern part of Washington Territory. By that fall Boise Basin was the center of population in the new territory and Idaho City (then called Bannock City) had passed Portland to become the largest town in the Pacific Northwest, with 6,275 inhabitants. Placerville had 3,254, Centerville, 2,638, Pioneer City, 2,743, and Granite Creek about 1,500. Never since have these communities come close to the numbers they had in 1863. By 1870, when the first decennial census of Idaho was taken, Idaho City's population had declined to only 889, Pioneer City's to 477, Centerville's to 474, Placerville's to 318, and Granite Creek's to 299. Buena Vista Bar, included in the 1863 estimate with Idaho City, was counted at 880 in 1870, but the combined total for the two (1,769) was less than a third of 1863's population.

The following table shows the dramatic decline of the Basin's population between 1863 and 1890:

	1863	1870	1880*	1890
IDAHO CITY	6,275	889	600	459
PLACERVILLE	3,254	318	200	173
PIONEER	2,743	477	200	137
CENTERVILLE	2,638	474	200	142

*Estimated

4.
Early placer miners sometimes used a "cradle" or "rocker" to separate gold from gravel.

5.
Gilbert Butler, who took this 1875 view of Idaho City, was called "the best teacher in Idaho Territory" by Bishop Daniel Tuttle.

6.
Boise Basin and surrounding country as depicted in an 1865 map published in San Francisco.

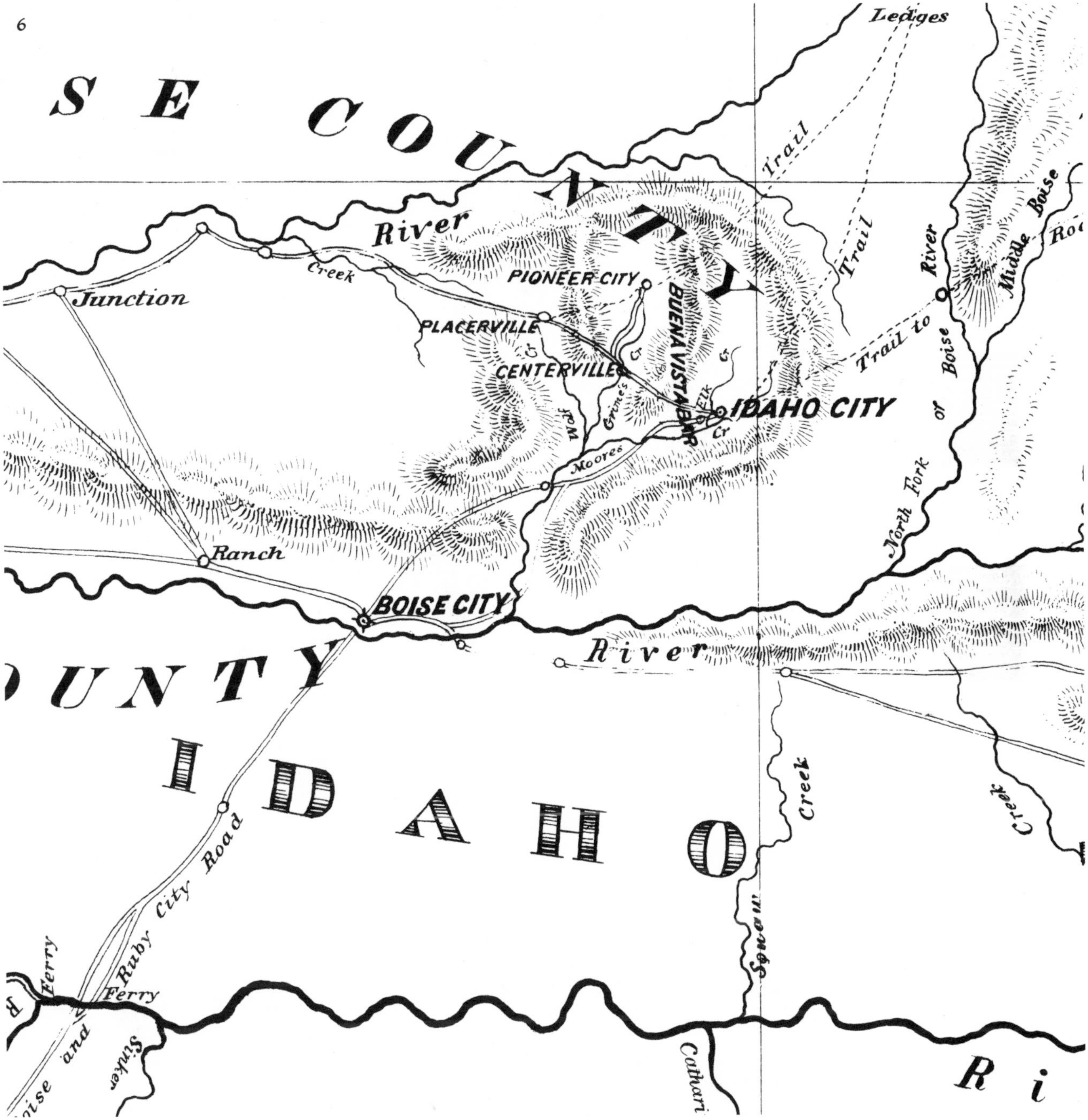

S E   C O U N T Y

River

Creek

Junction

PIONEER CITY

Trail

Trail

Trail to   River   Boise

Ledges

Middle Boise

Middle Roc

PLACERVILLE

CENTERVILLE

BUENA VISTA BAR

Elk   Cr.

Grimes's   Cr.

IM

Moores

IDAHO CITY

North Fork or Boise

Ranch

BOISE CITY

River

Creek

Creek

O U N T Y

I D A H O

Ruby City Road

Ferry

Ferry

Snake and

oise

Squaw   Creek

Cathari

R i

The People

Life in Boise Basin between 1862 and 1890 centered around many of the same concerns that life does today: work, play, love, marriage, family, birth, illness and death. Where life was different, it was the conditions of the time that made it so, not the basic needs of men and women. There was more violence, less adequate medicine, more physical discomfort, and less educational opportunity. Transportation and communication were primitive by our standards. Politics were more partisan and newspaper editors more opinionated. Ethnic groups were more distinctive and unassimilated, and one of them, the Chinese, outnumbered American born residents of the Basin by a wide margin. Women were a very small minority in all Basin communities, with all of the attendant social consequences. Children and family life were enjoyed by only a few of the thousands of men in mining communities.

It is easy to think of all miners as ignorant and rough, but many were not. They came from a wide variety of backgrounds in many lands, and if not yet used to American culture, were well versed in their own. One white observer found the Chinese, for example, "not only intelligent but educated," and added "I have yet to see one who is unable to read and write." Other national groups brought special talents and interests to Basin life, notably the Germans with their musical skills.

Although a few Boise Basin pioneers came with capital to invest in mines or business, most had to work hard to provide themselves with the basic necessities of food, clothing, and shelter. They developed their own mining claims, went to work for others, or supplied a skill or trade the community needed. The 1870 census gives us a good idea of how men and women were employed in the mining camps of Boise Basin.

There were 26 butchers, 23 merchants, 23 store clerks, 21 blacksmiths, 20 hotel keepers, 17 cooks, 16 carpenters, 13 wood cutters, 12 sawmill operators, 11 teamsters, and 10 lumbermen. Saloon keepers outnumber all other occupations with 32, equal to the number of cooks and boarding house keepers in supplying life support to a largely male community. There were 8 brewers. Payette river valley, in the western part of Boise county, had 101 farmers and a dozen dairymen who helped supply food to their mountain neighbors in the Basin.

Professional men included 9 attorneys, 7 physicians, 3 engineers and 2 bankers. Two men admitted to being professional gamblers. Law enforcement was represented by a U.S. Marshall and his deputy, a County Sheriff and an Under Sheriff, 3 County Deputy Sheriffs, 2 jailers, and 3 night watchmen. There were 3 justices of the peace.

Trades, in addition to those mentioned earlier, were 6 barbers, 5 bakers, 3 cabinet makers, 3 tin smiths, 3 printers, 3 watch makers, 2 brick masons, 2 assayers, 2 tailors, and a painter, a photographer, a mill wright and a wagon maker. Unusual occupations included:

7.
A group of young people of Idaho City posed in solemn dignity for this early photograph. Women outnumber the men 17 to 4 in the picture, but in the total population it was the other way 'round.

charcoal burner, huckster, game hunter, and soda water manufacturer. Associated with mining were a ditch owner, 7 ditch overseers, and a quartz mill operator. Indicative of transportation modes of the time were 5 common carriers, 3 ox team drivers, an expressman, a freighter, 7 liverystable operators, 6 mule packers, 3 stage drivers, and a toll road keeper. There was also a Wells Fargo agent.

The vast majority of women listed in the 1870 census were "Keeping House," but there were a few who ran businesses or worked for wages. Jane Emerson, 35, who lived alone with an 8 year old son, took in washing and ironing. Four women were dress makers. Bridget Foye, an Irishwoman of 37 with three small children, ran a hotel. Her 33 year old husband was a miner. Julia McAuliff, also Irish, taught school. Jemima Neville, 39, a native of Virginia, took in boarders, as did Margaret Buckley, Irish, assisted by two teen-age daughters who waited on table. Ah Hong, 25, was Mrs. Buckley's Chinese cook. Four young Germans danced for a living in a Granite creek hurdy-gurdy house. Although 3 women were employed in James Davidson's Placerville hotel, the cooks were Chinese. Six women in the Basin were listed as prostitutes, but there were probably more.

Countries represented in the Basin's population, in order of numbers, were China, Ireland, Germany, Azores Islands, Canada, England, Norway, France, Scotland, Switzerland, Austria-Hungary, Mexico, Denmark, Sweden, Sandwich Islands, Wales, Russia, Greece and Finland. (There were more Chinese than all other foreign-born combined). Most surprising, and as yet unexplained, is the large number of Portuguese miners from the Azores Islands in the North Atlantic Ocean. All of them lived at Pioneerville, and were described in 1867 as "sober, steady, upright men, with not a pauper or 'bummer' among them."

The Basin was a young man's world, by and large, for not only were there few women and children, but very few older men. It was a time and a place for the able-bodied who could do the heavy work of placering and quartz mining. The 1870 census lists 6 men who were 60 years old, and only 8 who were older. This is less than one percent of the total male white population. There were probably no Chinese over 60.

Of the children in Boise Basin in 1870 about half (187) were born in Idaho. There were 63 from California and 57 from Oregon. These statistics tell us where families had lived before coming to Idaho. Other natal states of Basin children, in order of numbers, were Missouri, New York, Massachusetts, Iowa, Montana, Wisconsin, Illinois, Louisiana, Washington, Indiana, Minnesota, Nevada, South Carolina, Pennsylvania, and Virginia. There were only 7 foreign born children in the Basin in 1870; 3 from Germany, 2 from New Brunswick, and one each from France and Scotland. The children growing up in the mining camps of Boise Basin in 1870 lived in a world very different from that of their contemporaries in just about any other section of the United States, with a mixture of races, nationalities, and ages that was unique.

8.
Butchers at work in an Idaho City shop. Cattle, hogs and sheep were driven live to Basin towns and slaughtered there.

9.
These Idaho City pioneers gathered in front of Nat Howse's Idaho City saloon to have their picture taken. They came from many lands.

10.
Brass lamps and ornate wallpaper decorated the lobby of Idaho City's Luna House, the Basin's largest hotel. It burned down in 1927.

11.
These elegantly dressed young women, most of them married, represented the gentler aspect of Basin life. Women took the lead in church, social and charitable activities.

Getting There

Travel into Boise Basin in the fall of 1862, in the rush following the initial discovery of gold on Grimes creek. was either on foot or horseback. Heavy supplies were carried by pack animals. Hundreds of the hopeful came with what they could carry on their backs — a blanket roll, a little food, a gun (for hunting or self-protection), spare clothing, and very little else.

A few old hands, with experience in earlier gold rushes, loaded pack strings of horses, mules or donkeys and made their first trip in with tools, flour and other staples for resale. Anything they could deliver to the new region, including the animals, could be sold for several times what they had paid or borrowed to get started. Many who would later become established business men and community leaders acquired their first significant capital that way.

By the spring and summer of 1863 the really big rush to the Basin was on. Nearly all who came that year, and the tons of food and supplies they needed to live and start mining, came up the Columbia river. Oregon Steam Navigation Company paddle wheel steamboats ran from Portland to the Dalles, passengers and freight were hauled around the falls by land to another steamer that carried them to Umatilla or Wallula. John Hailey and William Ish began running saddle trains that spring, over the Blue mountains to Grande Ronde valley, then by way of Baker valley and Burnt river to Snake river at Farewell Bend. Their path followed the Payette river to Horseshoe Bend, then went up Harris creek and over the divide into Boise Basin. Placerville was the first of the new towns to profit from being on this route, since all traffic to the Basin from the Columbia passed through there.

John Hailey described the saddle train business: "The owner of the train would furnish each passenger with a horse and a saddle so he could ride, would also pack a small amount of baggage for each person and furnish sufficient amount of substantial provisions for the trip, with the necessary cooking utensils. The passengers did the cooking in camp while the train-master looked after the animals, packing, etc. The fare for this trip was fifty dollars and each passenger was expected to pay in advance. Toll cost about ten dollars for the round trip for each animal, and added to this was the cost of the grub, the shoeing of the animals, the wages for the train-master, and frequently the loss of a horse or two. It took about fourteen days for the round trip and then the horses and trainmaster had to lay off for a week to rest from the hard trip, so it will be seen that all they took in was not clear profit."

In September, 1863, passenger traffic to the mines slacked off and Ish & Hailey switched to packing in supplies. They got from 16 to 25 cents per pound for hauling freight, which made it a good business. Until roads could be built, it was still the only way to get goods and supplies to the Basin. Many people left in the fall, since

12.
Before roads were built, or when wagons couldn't get through, packers supplied Boise Basin towns. Mules and donkeys were favored for this kind of transportation.

little mining or prospecting could be done in winter. The population of Boise Basin ebbed and flowed with the seasons as miners and merchants sought milder climate for the winter months.

In the sping of 1864 thousands returned, and many were able for the first time to come part or all of the way by stagecoach. Three different lines were serving the Basin by summer, 1864.
Ish & Hailey's ad appeared June 18th: "New Line of Coaches Through from Placerville to Umatilla in Four Days!" Hailey recalled that the road was not passable over the whole of its 285 miles until the first of June. Earlier travelers were forced to switch to saddle trains to pass over some of the more difficult sections.

Ish & Hailey's competition for the Columbia river trade was Greathouse & Company. Greathouse had a mail contract and also hauled Wells Fargo & Company's express. This line followed a different road over the Blue mountains and met the steamboats at Wallula. Although Greathouse had many advantages, and was expected to drive Ish & Hailey out of business, "Uncle John" recalled with satisfaction, half a century later, how he had hung on

and outfoxed the opposition. He especially scorned his rival's use of California horses, noting that his own tough "half-breed horses of medium size that had been raised on bunch grass" could outdo the fancier breeds without having to be fed nearly as much expensive hay and grain. He also began to compete by hauling express and treasure at far lower rates, and still made a reasonable profit.

Ward & Company began a stage line between Idaho City and Boise City in the fall of 1864. It ran coaches on Mondays, Wednesdays and Fridays, leaving the City Hotel at 8 a.m. and arriving in Boise at 5 p.m. the same day. The return trip, on Tuesdays, Thursdays and Saturdays, took an hour longer, since it was uphill most of the way. After snow fell, the schedule was rarely met, but the people had to accept it. They also had to accept a great deal of discomfort, and on occasion sheer misery, to make the journey at all.

As the spring rush began again in 1865, an *Idaho World* correspondent from Placerville paid tribute to the stagecoach companies: "Of all men, I think the 'stagers' deserve the most credit, in opening for us a public highway to the 'Lower Regions', — pardon me — I mean to Walla Walla, Wallula, and Umatilla, thereby aiding greatly the development of Idaho."

Parts of the route, and various bridges and ferry boats along the way, were built and maintained by private parties under license from the County commissioners, but most of it was the responsibility of the stagecoach operators. They had to build stations every 10 or 12 miles where fresh teams could be substituted for tired ones, maintain barns for shelter and hay for feeding the animals. They paid company employees to man these lonely

13.
Today the Boise Basin Museum, these brick buildings at Wall and Montgomery streets, Idaho City, date from 1867. They were built and operated by James A. Pinney as a book store, post office, and stage stop.

Greathouse & Co.'s
STAGES
—between—
BOISE BASIN & WALLULA
—carrying the—
U. S. MAIL
..AND..
WELLS, FARGO & CO.'S
EXPRESS !
LEAVE the International Hotel, Placerville,
Every Other Day at one o'clock, P. M. 27tf

Through in 48 Hours!!

NEW LINE
OF
COACHES
THROUGH
FROM
PLACERVILLE TO UMATILLA
IN
FOUR DAYS!

ISH & HALEY's Coaches leave the Empire Hotel,
Placerville, every other day, for Umatilla.
ISH & HALEY, Proprietors.
Placerville, June 18th, 1864. 38tf

Idaho & Boise City
STAGE LINE.

WARD & CO.'S Stages leave Idaho City TRI
WEEKLY, on Mondays, Wednesdays and
Fridays, at 8 o'clock a. m., arriving in Boise city
at 5 o'clock p. m., same day. Returning, leave
Boise city at 7 a. m., on Tuesdays, Thursdays and
Saturdays, and arrive in Idaho city at 5 p. m. All
Packages, &c., entrusted to them will be promptly
delivered. Office at the City Hotel, Idaho. 37tf

14.
*Stage company ads from the
Idaho World, 1864, stressed
speed, not comfort, since there
really wasn't any.*

outposts, some of which were scheduled as meal stops for the
passengers. Families usually operated the stations where food was
served, and women and children were sometimes in peril from
Indian raids. (Undoubtedly Indian women and children were in a lot
more danger from white attacks, however. Hundreds of them were
killed by white raiders in southern Idaho in the 1860s as miners and
ranchers moved in).

To run a successful stage business over many years, as John Hailey
and other pioneer operators did, required great organizational skill
and dedication. It was a complicated business, with intense
competition and unexpected problems to be dealt with. Storms could

make roads impassable at any time — not just in winter. Accidents and breakdowns were common, as were holdups. Indian attacks, though rare, usually resulted in livestock driven off and barns and stage stations burned.

Few people today can even imagine the hardships of stage travel in the 1860s. Even in good weather roads were so rough that passengers took a constant pounding. "One can hardly realize the wonderful structure and adaptablility of the human frame to the exigency of all conditions," wrote J.B. Wright in 1875, "until after a ride across the lava beds of the Snake river desert in a stage coach."

The toll road from Idaho City to Boise City over the summit between More's creek and Cottonwood creek was especially difficult in winter. In 1870 it was owned by Judge Milton Kelly, later publisher and editor of the *Idaho Tri-Weekly Statesman*. After *World* editor George Ainslie had been forced to join other passengers in wielding shovels for an hour in order to get the stagecoach through one especially bad stretch, he angrily asked "Why does not the wealthy proprietor of this road take efficient measures to repair such places?"

One of the conditions for receiving a license to operate and collect toll on these roads was that they be properly maintained. Licenses were for a maximum of five years, and could be revoked if maintenance was not adequate. Tolls authorized for the Idaho City-Boise City road were: "For each wagon, sleigh or vehicle with one span or one yoke of animals, $1.00; for each additional span or yoke, .50; riding animals, each, .25; pack or loose animals, each, .15; hogs or sheep, each, .05." Proprietors paid an annual license fee of $50.00 and put up a bond of $500.00.

Boise County's commissioners established a county road district in 1865 and appointed a supervisor. Every able bodied man was assessed an annual road tax of one dollar. By 1879, when there were eight districts, the commissioners received 24 sealed bids from men seeking the annual contracts to maintain them. These maintenance districts were in addition to the toll roads for which private contractors were responsible, and for which they paid annual license fees.

Citizens often had to supply their own maintenance, however, if they wanted to keep the roads open. In March, 1865, 50 Pioneerville men stomped through six feet of snow to Centerville and back, a distance of 16 miles, to break the trail for vehicles. They facetiously dubbed themselves the "Hog'em Traveling Club."

Spring travel in the mountains was usually the most difficult. Surprisingly, winter travel was often the easiest. When there was a good roadbed of packed snow sleighs replaced stagecoaches. They made good time with less bone jarring than wheeled vehicles over rutted and rocky roads. By December in most years runners had

15.
Matthew G. Luney's famous Luna House as it appeared in an 1890 engraving. It was located at the corner of Montgomery and Commercial streets, Idaho City. The hotel opened in 1868 with 25 rooms, but was nearly doubled in size in 1879.

replaced wheels throughout the basin. Sleighs went as far as they could on roads to the outside, and were replaced by stages at the first station after the snow got too thin to carry them.

Old timers seem to have enjoyed winter travel, as a January, 1867, account suggests: "There is good sleighing now all over the country. Billy Hise makes the trip to Boise City a fine sleigh ride all the way; Pinkham's line to Centerville, Placerville, and Pioneer City is a pleasure trip; and Dryde's hourly line to and from the Warm Springs, in that fine large sleigh, comfortably provided with warm robes, is a great luxury to our city folks who can indulge in the short ride...Sleighing is a good thing for a little while."

In 1869,Pinkham's "splendid and comfortable high-geared sleighs" were running around the Basin daily, and drew the comment that "the ride is worth double the fare during this fine sleighing season." A winter dance in any Boise Basin town usually attracted people from other towns who came by sleigh. Many accounts speak with delight of the silvery jingle of the bells, of singing and merriment.

The Railroad Era

After the transcontinental railroad was completed in May, 1869, significant changes took place in the way the Basin was supplied. The Columbia river route was gradually supplanted by new freight roads from points on the railroad. San Francisco goods came by train to Winnemucca where they were transferred to freight wagons for the trip north. Eastern shipments were transferred at Kelton, Utah. This caused a reduction in freight rates to Idaho, leading the *Idaho World* to take an editorial poke at the Oregon Steam Navigation Company for its "short-sighted, selfish and grasping policy" during the years it had a monopoly on trade to the Basin. "The great inland trade route to Idaho is being fast diverted from a route which is under control of a soul-less corporation, built up and enriched by the gold fields of Idaho."

In July, 1869, a Centerville merchant was able to advertise "First by Railroad, New Goods...by way of the Central Pacific Railroad to Winnemucca, and from there to Centerville by mule trains." The Kelton Road, over which most of the freight came, was about 50 miles shorter than the Umatilla route, and followed less difficult terrain most of the way.

Another change was noted by the *World*:

> In the early days of this camp a considerable portion of the supplies required came from Salt Lake valley, and it was not an unusual thing to see Latter Day Saints — laymen, bishops and apostles, — bull-whacking through our streets, vending their vegetables, eggs, butter and salt. By the improvement of transportation facilities and the cultivation of the rich valleys of the Territory they were gradually crowded back, and for a long time have seldom been seen. Lately, however, by the completion of the overland railroad and the consequent changes in the channel of trade, the services of the Saints are again brought into use as freighters.

Although pack trains continued to operate in Idaho after roads were built, they usually could not compete directly with freight wagons. Packers were limited by the relatively small load each individual animal could carry. Wagons could haul larger weights more efficiently, and by putting eight, ten or more teams out front, could pull three heavy wagons in tandem, using only one man as driver. Oxen and mules were favored for this kind of tough pulling, since strength and steadiness were more important than speed. There continued to be a need for packers, however, since new gold discoveries were being made well into the 20th Century. Until roads could be built, pack animals were the only means of getting supplies through the mountains to these isolated outposts. When the wagon roads were impassible with mud, snow, or ice, even older districts like Boise Basin called on the packers to keep them supplied.

16.
Idaho City in about 1890 was a town of 459 people. Its brick and wooden buildings were neat and well kept.

17.
This crowd gathered in front of Chris Meffert's Centerville Hotel to pose for the photographer. His saloon was open seven days a week, and was a social center for the small mining town.
(See page 73).

Celestials

The Chinese played a significant part in the history of Boise Basin. When the 1870 federal census was taken 1,751 of Boise County's people were Chinese — more than 45% of the total. By 1880 the area's declining mining economy had reduced the total county population to 1,970, and 1,125 of them were Chinese — well over 60%.

Chinese had worked the mines of California for years before the 1862 discovery of gold in the Basin. Thousands helped build the transcontinental railroad, completed at Promontory Point, Utah, on May 10, 1869. But even before the linking of the Central Pacific and Union Pacific created a surplus of Oriental workers in the West, thousands of them had already made their way to the mining camps of Idaho.

In an item headlined "John's First Appearance," the *Idaho Tri-Weekly Statesman* gave this account:

"That interesting sight so familiar to old Californians, of long trains of celestials on the move in single file, supporting the middle of their long-handled shovels or a bamboo stick with pendant sacks of rice, chop sticks, rockers, and gum boots, filed among Idaho street yesterday morning, to the great amusement of lookers on..."
The People of Boise City who watched the passage of the Chinese on their way to Idaho City on September 13, 1865, little realized that they were witnessing a significant moment in Idaho history. For many people present that day, these were the first Orientals they had ever seen. A few Chinese had arrived in Boise Basin in 1864, and were working as domestic servants, common laborers, or taking in laundry, but organized Chinese immigration was just beginning. An *Idaho World* correspondent from Pioneer City wrote in late September, 1865, that "the Chinamen are coming among us. Lord deliver us from the 'Locusts of Egypt!' They devour all before them." In a more philosophical mood he added, "If destiny has so shaped it, let them come."

Come they did, and by early October the *World* noted that "between fifty and sixty Chinamen are reported to be at work on claims lately purchased by them on More's creek, below the tollgate. This is the first gang, we believe, which has ventured into that line of business in this portion of the country."

A writer in the *Capital Chronicle* of Boise recalled in 1869 that a Chinese agent named Billy Hy had obtained permission in the summer of 1865 "to purchase mining ground, and the privilege of peaceable mining was granted by white miners to the Chinese." This observer dated the beginning of Chinese placer mining on More's creek to August, 1865, several weeks before the *World* noticed it. He said that by December there were about 150 Chinese in Idaho City and vicinity and that Chinese gambling houses and brothels had been opened.

That Chinese in the Basin had become well established in laundry

18.
Idaho City Chinese maintained their own language, customs and dress as best they could. This scene was in a Chinese neighborhood, but the enterprising Orientals owned property thoughout the town.

work before they were able to start mining in the summer of 1865 is indicated by George Owens' 1864 business directory. Owens listed Hop Ching, Quong Hing, Fan Hop, Sam Lee and Song Lee as running laundries in Idaho City. Buena Vista Bar, which would have the Basin's largest Chinese population in a few years, had none in 1864, but at Placerville Sing Sam had a laundry, and one Lee Sin was in business both there and at Centerville. This competition naturally led to a loss of income for the Basin's laundresses, several of whom were widows.

By November, 1865, the Chinese presence in the Basin was significant. "Their celestial countenances begin to adorn every portion of the terrestrial scene," said the *World*. ". . . nearly every day they are spilled out of wagons like so much general merchandise." The number of Chinese in the mines of the Basin had probably reached a thousand by 1867. The camps now had

Chinatowns and Chinese merchants who imported a wide variety of goods from the Orient. Well-financed Chinese companies had bought up many of the older placer claims and were re-working them with coolie labor. White mine owners also began hiring the Chinese, at wages substantially lower than they had to pay white miners.

This was viewed with disgust by most older inhabitants, and an already strong anti-Chinese sentiment grew in bitterness. The *Idaho Tri-weekly Statesman* said, "We hear but one remark about Idaho City, and that is 'The Chinamen have got it.' There is no use grumbling about the Johns any more, for they are evidently not going to stop until the Boise county mines are all worked over again." The *World* thought "Idaho has already more than enough of Chinamen. Our mines ought to be worked by white men. Coolies will ruin any mining company they flock to..." Harassment of the docile and hard-working Orientals became a common feature of life in Boise Basin. Chinese "washed claims which the white man had abandoned as paid out, and were satisfied with profits of two or three dollars a day," recalled Thomas Donaldson. "They worked more hours than any miners I ever saw and, poor souls, were often the victims of Christian (?) extortion and discriminations... Resistance to white men was the last thing a Chinaman dared."

In December, 1864, the Second Territorial Legislature had shown its racial bias by passing a law requiring "all Mongolians, whether male or female, of whatever occupation, to pay a license tax of four dollars for each and every month they reside in this territory." In January, 1866, this monthly tax was raised to five dollars. The Chinese were supported in their appeal of these discriminatory acts by a number of white leaders who got them repealed in 1869. As Donaldson explains, the tax was bad enough, but "white loafers, hard up for cash, would procure blank licenses, visit the diggings under the guise of license collectors, and poor John would be threatened and bullied until he handed over four dollars..." — sometimes for the third or fourth time.

Beatings and murders of Chinese by whites were not uncommon, usually by "persons unknown," who went unpunished. (Even mining camp children found the peaceful Orientals fair game for milder forms of persecution and practical jokes. In March, 1879, the *World* said, "Snowballing is the favorite amusement here, much to the disgust of almond-eyed John.")

On September 27, 1865, a Chinese laundryman was shot to death by a white man in Idaho City, prompting Editor H. C. Street to observe: "The Chinese in Idaho (City) are very harmless and very industrious, and I will venture to say that such is not the character of the man, whoever he is, that kills one of them when there is no provocation... To kill a Chinaman, or a defenseless woman, or to strangle a canary bird — one is about as brave an act as another."

19.
"Chinamen's House" was the caption given to this 1884 lithographic detail in Elliott's History of Idaho Territory.

20.
World Editor H. C. Street thought it cowardly for anyone to kill "harmless" and "industrious" Chinese.

21.
Idaho City's Chinese community celebrated this wedding in style and had a photographer record the event.

Hiram Kurtz, who did the shooting, was placed in the county jail to await trial. In November, 1865, he was convicted of murder in the first degree and sentenced to hang. Governor Caleb Lyon commuted this to life imprisonment in January, 1866, but the condemned man barely escaped the noose anyway. His brother carried the Governor's order from Boise to Idaho City in a blinding snow storm, just making it in time. In April, 1867, Kurtz was one of four prisoners who escaped from the county's rather porous jail. One was killed, but Kurtz and the others were re-captured.

Governor David Ballard pardoned him in September, 1868, after receiving a petition signed by "nearly all" of the citizens of Idaho City.

If the Chinese were patient and timid where white mistreatment was concerned, they were hardly that among themselves. Violence between individual Chinese and between rival companies was often reported in the papers, as when "Ah Chung, Ah Kum, and Ah Fung, living near Centerville, engaged in the innocent pastime of hanging one of their countrymen for the purpose of making him 'come out' with about $500 which they claimed he had of theirs in his possession . . ." He was rescued by a passer-by, and two of his attackers arrested. The third ran away.

Nearly all Chinese in Boise Basin came from the neighborhood of Canton. Most were from the Pearl River delta and hence members of a regional district association called Sze-yap, usually written "See Yup" in early Idaho newspapers. Members of the Sze-Yap were apt to be poor peasants with little or no education. The rival Yung wa association (often written "Yen Wah" or "Chung wa") was made up of better educated members of the merchant class. Both organizations were instrumental in bringing Cantonese labor to America in a well-developed system that advanced the individual worker the cost of his passage and board — a loan he had to pay off before he could save money for himself.

All Chinese who came to Idaho in gold rush days expected to return to their homeland. Young men hoped to save enough money from their hard work in the mines to return relatively well-off, marry and raise families. Middle aged men had often left wives and children behind when they came to America. They sent money home as often as they could, but all longed for the day when they could return to what they called the Celestial Empire. The associations that brought Chinese workers to America continued to look out for them in time of need, providing medical and legal service, and seeing that their bones were neatly packaged and shipped back to China if they died here.

The See Yups and the Yen Wahs had a pitched battle on Elk Creek in September, 1870, over water rights for placer mining. Using "shovels, sluice forks, knives and other weapons" they inflicted fearful damage on each other until the bloodshed was stopped and thirteen of them were arrested by Deputy Sheriff Joseph Rowe. At the hearing, a bit of legal trickery took place that the *World* thought very amusing. In what it called the "Doctrine of Substitution," the paper described what happened when the Chinese miners were herded into court "for participating in the innocent amusement of scalping each other with shovels and prodding each other with sluice forks." Their attorney found that one of his clients had not appeared and there was danger that his bail bond would be lost. "As Chinamen all look so much alike that it is difficult to tell one from another...he immediately procured another Chinaman to appear in place of the absentee...all of which the Court and the District Attorney were, of course, ignorant of..."

This white notion that "all Chinamen look alike," is as old as relations between the races. It is reflected in a number of frontier anecdotes that suggested that if you couldn't catch and punish one Chinese for a crime, any other Chinese would do. In the See Yup-Yen Wah case, described here, the judge dismissed them all, so the substitution was not noticed.

Murders of Chinese by other Chinese were not unknown, but there is no record of a Chinese killing a white man in Boise Basin. There were ten natives of China in the Territorial penitentiary at Idaho

22.
Most Boise Basin hotels and restaurants employed Chinese cooks in the 19th Century, as did some cattle ranches and prosperous townspeople.

23.
Every other face you saw in Boise Basin in early days might be Chinese. Buena Vista Bar had 733 natives of China in 1870 and only 147 whites.

24.
The Boise County Jail doubled as Territorial Penitentiary until 1872 when most prisoners were transferred to a new institution in Boise City.

City in 1870 — a small number out of the 1,752 Chinese in the Basin. (There were five Irish and one each of Russian, English, Welsh and Swedish prisoners, and five American-born convicts. Most Chinese were serving time for petit larceny and other minor crimes. All of those in prison for murder and crimes of violence in 1870 happened to be white.) Killing a man on the Idaho frontier rarely meant having to hang for it. A good lawyer and friendly witnesses almost invariably secured an acquittal on grounds of self-defense. There also seems to have been a tendency for white judges to let the Chinese work out their own disputes, so long as no white interests were involved. Chinese punishment of transgressions committed by one member of their race against another were apt to be cruel and bloody. The white community may have shuddered a bit, but did not interfere.

Chinese life and celebrations seemed totally alien and incomprehensible to the white population at first, but over the years gradually became an accepted part of life in the Basin. Westerners found the Chinese custom of setting off fireworks at funerals strange indeed, but came to look forward to Chinese New Year's festivities. "The Chinese are very hospitable on their holidays," observed the *World* in 1885, "and treat those of the 'Melican' race who call on them with the best they have, and are always pleased to receive calls. A large number of people of this place, both ladies and gentlemen, made New Year's calls last Saturday and were hospitably treated."

A *World* correspondent, writing from Boston, on Grimes creek, in February, 1879, said "The Chinese are still celebrating their New Year, and a few days ago invited us to attend one of their feasts. We cannot speak in the highest terms of Celestial diet, as the only really palatable thing to be had on the occasion was brandy." After bravely downing half a dozen "grub worms, of a pale yellowish color...and not wishing to appear disagreeable," the writer described his reaction thus: "A peculiar kind of gone-ness came over the spirit of our dreams, a green mildew gathered on our brow, great drops of cold perspiration stood out in bold relief on our venerable...forehead."

For the February, 1870 funeral of Chinese merchant Lee Pow's bookkeeper, the Idaho City brass band was hired "to discourse the Dead March from Saul, Mozart's Twelfth Mass, or some other doleful requiem."

By the 1880s children of the few Chinese merchants lucky enough to have wives and families were attending Idaho City's public school. The *World* commented on the talents and cleverness of some of them, suggesting a degree of acceptance by that time. Ah Hing, American born, was asked by a fellow pupil if he was an American. The paper thought his reply witty: "Noke. Half China and Half United States." A map of the United States, executed by the daughter of a Chinese merchant, was proudly shown by her teacher to the *World* editor. He proclaimed it a "finely executed piece of artistic work."

25.
Sun Yow Loy was the fourth son of a Placerville Chinese family.

26.
Educated Chinese like Kum Ah Moe had a special role in relations between the races. This ad ran in the Idaho World.

27.
A well known figure on the streets of Idaho City was this Chinese vegetable farmer. He delivered fresh produce door to door.

28.
Placerville's I.O.O.F. Hall was one of that town's imposing buildings until it was destroyed by fire.

25

26

Blacks in Boise Basin

Throughout the goldrush era Boise Basin had a small but stable black population. George Owens' 1864 directory lists a total of 15 "colored" residents — exactly the same number U.S. Census takers found in 1870. Despite the *Idaho World's* fears, expressed editorially in 1865, that "without legislation (to prohibit it) the whole North will soon be swarming with free negroes," no such immigration into the Basin occurred.

Of seven blacks in Idaho City in 1864, three were listed as working in "shaving and hair cutting saloons" and one in "bathing rooms." Mrs. Maria Green, the only black woman in the Basin, worked at the Magnolia Restaurant. The occupation of the other two men was not listed. Centerville's two blacks, Peter Lee and J. M. Whitefield, ran a "hairdressing saloon," as did three of four Placerville black men, and Pioneerville's only one. But one man of the race is listed as a "miner," at a time when over 90% of the Basin's population was engaged in mining.

Blacks in Boise Basin were predominantly employed in the skilled and specialized occupation of barbering. An 1866 business directory indicates that 8 of the 12 "hair dressers" in Basin towns were black men. In 1870, no Basin town had more than four black residents, and the majority of those were barbers.

Mining

"The mines are being worked by night as well as by day. On account of the scarcity of water, it becomes necessary to use it at all times, and as many times over as possible," wrote Charles Nelson Teeter to the folks back home on June 1, 1864. "It is rather delightful to step out late in the evening, and view the light of a hundred fires that shine on every side, to light the miner in his search for gold."

This eye-witness account delineates clearly the chief limitation to successful placer mining in Boise Basin — the availability of water. The gold dust was there in surprising richness, throughout the region, mixed with the ancient sands and gravels of stream beds, banks, and bars. It took running water to wash it out. In a good placer year water was available over many months, from the first spring thaws into late summer or fall. An early spring was only good if the thaw was gradual. If the snowpack melted too fast destructive floods and a short season could be the result.

Getting the water from streams to the gravel to be washed required the building of elaborate ditch systems. *Nemo*, writing in the *Capital Chronicle* in 1869, said "There were not less than fifty miles of large first-class water ditches completed with necessary flumes in (full) operation by the spring of 1864...vital arteries of mining in many localities." He figured that a million dollars worth of ditches had been built to supply Basin placers by 1869. Some large ditch owners made fortunes on the water they sold to small operators with dry claims.

Washing large tonnages of sand and gravel in the most efficient way possible in the shortest possible time was the objective. Individuals might, in exceptionally good ground, get rich washing gravel in rockers or sluice boxes, but large scale hydraulic mining required the delivery of lots of water to a point high above the work. Water was piped down from ditches to small-apertured nozzles called "giants," where it was forced at enormous pressure into jets with the power to wash away whole mountains of gravel. The material was then washed through cleated sluice boxes that trapped the heavier gold particles.

Quartz mining in the Basin began early, but remained less productive than placering, primarily because of the much greater capital required for development. Digging tunnels or shafts into mountainsides, following ledges or veins of gold-bearing ore, was costly, with very high risks for investors. What looked good on the surface could peter out too soon — after tens of thousands or even hundreds of thousands had been spent on labor and machinery. Given the transportation of the day, getting stamp mills into position to do their work of crushing ore was enormously expensive. Twenty or more oxen or mules might make up a team dragging steam engines, boilers, stamp batteries, and other machine parts hundreds of miles over rough country. The fact that several of

29.
The awesome force of hydraulic giants can be seen in this view of placer mining near Idaho City.

the early mills were sold, relocated, and resold more than once tells us what a gamble it was.

Since one of the duties of early newspapers was "to build up the country," the pages of the *Idaho World* are filled with glowing accounts of new quartz discoveries, each needing only investment capital to make millionaires of their owners and backers. The Gold Hill mine at Quartzburg was one of the few lode mines in the Basin to be consistently productive and profitable. By the 1890s it had produced more than $2 million. Other famous quartz mines with significant early production were the Gambrinus and the Elk Horn, five and ten miles, respectively, above Idaho City.

Of the Basin's total gold production of more than $100 million by 1942, quartz mining accounts for a relatively small part. (For a detailed descripton of mining in Boise Basin see Merle W. Wells' *Gold Camps and Silver Cities*, second edition, 1983).

GOLD HILL MINE & WORKS,
Quartzburgh, Boise Co. Idaho.

30.
The Gold Hill was Boise Basin's most famous and productive lode mine. The town of Quartzburg grew up nearby, although not included in this 19th century lithograph.

31.
Margaretta F. Brown, wife of attorney Jonas W. Brown, was Idaho City's most accomplished amateur artist.

32.
Mrs. Brown's painting of hydraulic mining is her best known work. It has been reproduced in many books on Western history.

GRAVEL ELEVATOR. BEN WILLSON & G.W. CRANSTON PATENTED.

PLACERVILLE

BIRD'S EYE VIEW OF GRIME'S CREEK AND VICINITY. SHOWING A PORTION OF MINING AND OTHER PROPERTY OF BEN WILLSON PIONEERVILLE IDAHO TERR.

● GOLD SIGNATURE.

33.
This 1884 lithographic "bird's eye view" of Grimes creek gives some idea of the magnitude of Ben Willson's placer mining empire. His ditches and flumes supplied much of the water used by miners in the area.

34.
Quartzburg in its heyday was a thriving community of more than a hundred people. Today it has all but vanished.

35

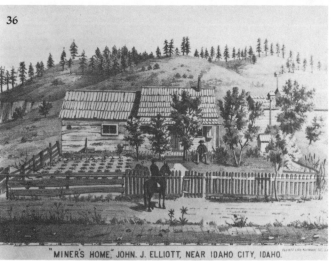

"MINER'S HOME," JOHN. J. ELLIOTT, NEAR IDAHO CITY, IDAHO.

35.
The great size of some hydraulic giants is shown by this picture of 14 men posed at the business end of one.

36.
The artist who illustrated Elliott's 1884 history found John J. Elliott's neat cabin and fenced yard a picturesque subject.

37

37.
The old town of Pioneerville was threatened by hydraulic mines that washed away its site near the end of the century.

38.
Kenna P. Plowman was one of the large scale placer miners in the Basin in the 1880s and after.

38

K. P. PLOWMAN'S MINING CLAIM, NEAR IDAHO CITY.

Rites of Passage

Births, weddings, anniversaries, and deaths were occasions for special ceremony or celebration in early Idaho. The *Idaho World* reported most of them — sometimes with detail that makes us feel a part of the scene, sharing the emotions of others who were there. We feel the delight of a proud father when we read this account by *World* editor George Ainslie in March, 1870:

> Born — to the better half of the editor of this paper, and to himself, on the outgoing of the month of February, A.D. 1870, a Daughter. The little stranger "Blooms in beauty, like a rose upon the parent stem." Do our readers think, or imagine we, the fond, the overjoyed, the indubitably happy paternal, after such a cri-sis could write anything muchly for this issue of the paper, or give attention muchly to duties editorial? Not muchly; and we shall give no other or further apology, either for what may be a-miss in this issue, for at home pretty much all is a Miss. Eleven and one-half pounds of beautiful baby! Only think of it and phancy our pheelinx!

The wedding of Jacob Wagner and Emma Bullock at Quartzburg in February, 1885, produced this pleasant word picture:

39

> The parlor and dining rooms were beautifully decorated with evergreens and artificial flowers. On the left wall of the dining room the letters J and E were artistically formed in evergreens, while the word "Welcome" graced the north wall. A large wedding bell was suspended from the ceiling of the parlor under which the happy couple were tied for life. At about 8:30 o'clock Mrs. F. F. Church played the wedding march on the organ and the bridal party entered the room... After the marriage ceremony the Christening of Mrs. J. H. Hawley's child took place... The child was named after the bride and President-elect Cleveland.

(Mrs. F. F. Church was the grandmother of Senator Frank Church. Mrs. J. H. Hawley was the wife of the distinguished pioneer attorney who would later be elected mayor of Boise and Governor of Idaho. The baby was named Emma Cleveland Hawley.)

> After the usual kissing and congratulations were offered the party repaired to the dining room where a grand feast was spread... after supper the guests were invited to the dance hall and a jolly good time was had until morning, when all bade Mr. and Mrs. Wagner adieu, wishing them health, happiness and success with their new life.

Funerals were reported in detail only if the deceased was a well-known leader in one of the Basin communities, or if the circumstances were especially tragic. Unusually large funerals

39.
Mrs. James H. Hawley would later become one of Idaho's first ladies.

40.
The picturesque cemetery at Placerville contains the graves of two of Mrs. Hawley's little boys. Many of the Basin's pioneers are memorialized on its white marble monuments.

41.
Anna Galbreaith. Her death in a wagon crash in 1879 was a tragedy to the entire community.

recorded were those of popular J. Marion More, a leading miner killed in a Silver City gunfight in 1868; of Sumner Pinkham, ex-sheriff, killed at the Warm Springs by Ferd Patterson in 1865; of E. D. Holbrook, former territorial representative in Congress, killed in a shoot-out with Charles Douglass in 1870, and of Mary Pinney, 25, wife of Postmaster James A. Pinney, who died suddenly at Idaho City in July, 1870. The death of the young is always especially touching, and the loss of 16 year old Anna Galbreaith in a fatal wagon crash September 27, 1879, affected the entire community. *World* editor E. W. Jones, who happened upon the scene of the accident shortly after, wrote this heart-rending account:

41

> One of the party approached us and told us that Anna was dead, that there had been an accident, that she had been thrown from the wagon and had broken her neck. Oh, how those words pierced the hearts of all! We went to the scene of the disaster, and raised the blanket from poor Anna's face...As we gazed upon the lifeless form, how hard to realize that it was Anna, who a short time before was making the woods ring with her merry laughter. The cheeks that were so rosy, and that were dimpled from the promptings of a pure, glad heart, were now pale in death...

Virtually the entire population of Idaho City filled the streets as Anna Galbreaith's body was brought into town. Her funeral was one of the largest in years — an occasion of grief for all, but especially for her brother Walter who was in the wagon when the tragedy happened.

Birthday parties and wedding anniversaries were other rites of passage described from time to time in the pages of early newspapers. They give us a feel for the texture of life in pioneer times and remind us that the important milestones were not basically different from those we celebrate today.

Christmas

Christmas in Boise Basin towns was a time especially dedicated to making the children happy. There were only 362 of them out of a total of 14,910 people in the Basin's four largest towns in 1863. Women were an equally cherished minority, numbering only 594, compared with 13,954 men, and it was the women who organized the Christmas festivities. Indeed, it is doubtful that Christmas would have been marked by much more than heavy saloon patronage were it not for "the civilizing influence of woman" so often noted in 19th century writings.

The women of Idaho City organized the town for a first class observance of the holiday in 1864. A large community Christmas tree was prepared, " bearing a present for someone on every branch. Persons wishing to contribute, or to present any person with a gift, can do so very pleasantly by attaching a card to the object and leaving it with the committee. It is understood that the tree has no connection with the church."

Merchants had stocked up on Christmas merchandise, and one enterprising retailer sold his supply of "Holiday presents, toys, furs, shawls and ladies' goods" at nightly auctions at the corner of Main and Wall streets. Public halls and sidewalks along the principal streets were adorned with evergreen boughs, symbols "of perpetual life." The ladies on the committee of arrangements were praised as "successful managers" of the holiday who "materially assisted in making the day and night a pleasant one." It was a day, said the paper, "without any disturbances of any kind. It was merry without excess, and happy with quiet content." For a town with 5,300 single men, this was indeed remarkable.

A Christmas tree and present-sharing at Placerville that year featured a visit from Santa Claus and "no little merriment, amounting at times to a perfect uproar" as gifts were opened. The day was made especially memorable in 1864 by a heavy snowfall that blanketed the Basin. For placer miners, dependent upon a good snow pack and runoff in the spring, this was a most welcome Christmas present.

42

J.W. Brown

Through the years, the celebration of Christmas continued to have the same focus: "There are but few 'little ones' in the aggregate of our population," said the *World* in 1866. "Let us make the holidays sweet and glad to them." The annual community Christmas tree party took place in the courthouse for many years. In 1878 Jonas W. Brown delivered a short talk to the children, "in which he called attention to the fact that all the young folks who attended the Christmas tree a year ago were present this time...It is seldom in a town with over a hundred small children that a year passes without a single death to record." After this solemn note, J.J. Mitchell played Santa Claus and passed out the presents. "He had on a good rig," noted the paper. "The children were all remembered."

42.
Jonas W. Brown was one of Idaho Territory's leading attorneys. He was active in temperance and Sunday School work.

The Christmas season for the adults in Basin towns was marked by dance parties and more formal holiday balls. The Masonic order frequently sponsored such events, but the commercial proprietors of dance halls sometimes offered their own. Church services were important in some years, as in 1869 when the Christmas tree party was followed by dancing until 11 p.m. when all adjourned to Idaho City's Catholic church for High Mass. "Father Mesplie officiated at the altar and Father Poulin presided at the choir, and such music as is heard on such occasions in the church is worth going to hear." Protestant musicians sometimes joined the Catholics for special services like this one.

New Year's

New Year's Eve and New Year's Day were annual occasions for much celebrating in the small mining communities of Boise Basin. In 1865, when Idaho City still had a population of several thousand people, there were two New Year's balls on the same night. Barney's Band played to "as many as there was room for" in Pickwick Hall and Paston's Quadrille Band accompanied an equally packed house at Magnolia Hall. (These dances were held on Monday, January 2, since New Year's fell on a Sunday that year). "A regular old fashioned watch meeting" was held at the Protestant Church in Idaho City on New Year's Eve, 1865, with Reverend Mr. Newton conducting. The service lasted from 10:30 until well after midnight.

On New Year's Night, 1865, Paston's Brass Band serenaded the town, "awakening all the yellow legged chickens and night owls of this neighborhood with the unusual melody. The band was out in full force and made the town vocal with its strains. A number of our citizens were recipients of their complimentary notice."

The day after New Year's was called "Ladies' Day" in 1869, and although it wasn't a leap year, offered an occasion for "a goodly number of the fair portion of our city..." to make "cheery calls upon the sterner sex at their dwellings and business places..." Since men outnumbered women seven to one in Boise Basin at the time, the men were delighted indeed to receive this attention. Their souls were gladdened by this "merry time of visiting" reported the *World.*

43

On January 1, 1870, the bachelors of Idaho City kept open house for the ladies — an event that Editor George Ainslie covered in detail:

> In company with our genial friend Jimmy Brown we called on Green White and Mike Fenner, at their residence, and though of the male persuasion, we were admitted and hospitably entertained by our young bachelor friends. Jimmy Brown had superintended the arrangement of the table, which groaned under the profuse display of all the delicacies of the season, while the sideboard was amply provided with wines and liquors of all kinds, suited to the taste of the most fastidious. Returning from there we called on that gay and festive young "bach" Harry Bowman, who was also keeping open house, and found a profuse supply of eatables and drinkables of all kinds, got up in a style that would have done credit to any of his lady callers.

Ainslie said he dared not visit any more of his bachelor friends, since they all would have insisted on his taking a drink and business prevented his indulging in a complete holiday.

The ladies of Idaho City turned out "in full force," reported Ainslie, "and none of the gentlemen who kept open house can complain of being neglected." Even the men who worked at the Territorial Penitentiary and the Wells Fargo express office opened their doors and spread their tables to receive women callers. Dave Wagner at the express office "was taken by a storm in the evening, and provided with suitable music, quite a bevy of young ladies and a number of young gentlemen finished up the festivities of the holidays by spending the night in dance and song...".

The women who visited Editor Ainslie at the *World* office found that he had nothing better than "printer's ink, paste, and coal oil to offer them." He promised to make amends for his negligence in some other manner in future. (Ainslie was a married man at the time. His young wife Sarah was expecting their second child, so he could be forgiven for not expecting callers on the day local bachelors held open house).

Some prankish Idaho City men prepared a special table for callers that day, composed of "a huge head of cabbage and an immense squash, together with a large joint of raw beef or soup bone, a plate full of raw potatoes and some other as appropriate side dishes." After enjoying their guests' astonishment and disappointment the jovial fellows led them into another room where the real feast was spread: "fruit, cakes, nuts and sweetmeats of all kinds with something to wash them down."

As the years went by and the population of the Basin dwindled to hundreds instead of thousands, New Years' celebrations became less

43.
Green White was a popular man-about-town in early Idaho City.

44.
Musicians like those in this unidentified group enlivened things at early dances and celebrations.

45.
Snows were deep and winters long in Idaho City. The house of Dr. Herman Zipf is at right.

44

varied and elaborate. Guns were fired and black powder was exploded at midnight, making pine-clad hills ring. Dances were held and congregations gathered in the churches to see the New Year in, just as they had before, but entertainment was more likely to be home-grown rather than professional as in the boom years.

A New Year's Eve dance at Centerville in 1886 attracted young people from Placerville and Pioneer as well as local residents. In the absence of a band, music was provided by "Mr. Edwards on the violin and Mr. Lippincott on the organ...anyone who could not dance to the music they made ought to go home and go to bed," wrote a correspondent. During a lull in the dancing two energetic young men amused the company "with some fine exhibitions of their proficiency in the abstruse science of leap frog which caused much merriment, though finally objected to by the ladies as being too utterly masculine." (Probably the young fellows had tippled a bit too freely and the women got tired of their oafish horseplay).

Although winter roads were bad that year they were not impassible. Disdaining the local dance, "a four-horse load of Centervillians" went to Emmettsville to the New Year's ball given there. Boise Basin people were used to winter travel, and went freely from one town to another to attend holiday dances. Often several sleigh-loads of couples set off together to go a dozen miles or more, dance all night, and return next morning, still singing to the merry jingle of the harness bells.

45

Independence Day

"The crack of rifles and pistols at night and the booming of thirty-five anvils in the morning woke the town to the Fourth of July." Thus did the *Idaho World* begin its description of the activities of July 4, 1866. The firing of anvils was a popular sport in early celebrations, achieved by placing a quantity of black powder on an anvil, inverting another anvil atop that, and lighting a fuse to the powder. The clanging boom and flying anvil that resulted was great fun.

Band music and a parade began in midmorning and, on this typical Idaho City Fourth of July, were followed by the reading of the Declaration of Independence and an oration. That evening a grand ball was held. The program varied from year to year, but these were traditional ways of marking the nation's birthday. Not traditional were some other things about that 1866 celebration.

First was the appearance in Emerald green uniforms of the Emmet Guards, a militant unit of the local Irish-American Fenian Circle, dedicated to the establishment of a Republic of Ireland. Fenianism was at its peak in the Basin that year. The Guards drilled with rifles, and had a shooting match at Buena Vista Bar later. Another unusual feature of 1866 was a Fourth of July oration that drew cat-calls and an angry response from a large part of the audience. The speaker had one strike against him before he even started: he was a Republican in a stronghold of Southern Democrats, but when his theme turned out to be "wholly devoted to the 'great cause' of Abolitionism, negro equality, and negro suffrage," his largely Southern audience was furious. "The grand amalgamation of all races and colors into one nationality, governed by one universal, equal Congressional and social law, embraced the speaker's idea of future national greatness," said the *World*. "At one point...where he demanded the ballot for the negro, a great crowd left the theater."

The ball, later that evening, was sponsored by the Fenian Brotherhood. A large crowd danced to the music of the Cosmopolitan Band at the Magnolia Hotel, then took a midnight supper at the City Hotel. The *World* proclaimed it "a brilliant and pleasant affair." In 1865 two balls were held in the Basin. Fisher's Hotel on Buena Vista Bar offered one on July 3 and another was held July 4 in the court house at Idaho City. The committee in charge included a number of men who would later become famous in Idaho: George Ainslie, Centerville attorney, later editor of the *Idaho World* and delegate in Congress; Orlando "Rube" Robbins, frontier marshall and chief scout in the Indian wars, and Jimmy Hart, Placerville saloon keeper whose humor delighted Boise for a generation after he moved there in 1874.

In 1869, temperance lodges were active in the Basin, but when the Good Templars of Centerville tried to organize a grand ball they

46.
The Fourth of July parade at Idaho City usually included the town's fairest maidens riding in a Liberty Car.

couldn't muster the support to make it worthwhile. The *World* was disgusted. "Inasmuch as our citizens have made no preparations to observe the coming anniversary, we feel it would be barely pertinent for us to devote more than this small space to (it)... In Turkey, do as the turkeys do."

July 4, 1870, was celebrated properly, with all of the traditional flourishes: band music, reading of the Declaration, a fine patriotic oration, and dancing. Since the events took place at the Warm Springs Resort south of town "the city during the day presented a rather deserted appearance as nearly all the business

houses were closed..." Jonas W. Brown, Samuel A. Merritt, and
Frank Miller were the speakers. The Idaho Brass Band supplied the
music. Dancing did not get started until after sundown, as it was
too warm earlier, even though Robert Turner, proprietor of the
Warm Springs had an arbor of pine and fir boughs built to supply
shade. During the heat of the day many took walks in the woods,
picked wild flowers, or courted. "Love sick couples whispered soft
nonsense in each other's ears," said the paper. Ice cream was had in
abundance, other refreshments were excellent, and especially notable
was the fact that there were no incidents or accidents and "not one
intoxicated individual was seen."

Other Basin Fourth of July observances were similar, and only
occasionally was there neither a reading of the Declaration of
Independence nor a patriotic speech. Flags were always flown and
black powder was exploded. Occasionally there were fireworks on
East Hill, purchased with contributions from individuals and
businesses. For the children of the towns the Fourth was always a
grand holiday. They often got to march in the parade with their
Sunday School classmates, and teen-age girls looked forward to
riding on a wagon heavily festooned with red, white and blue
bunting, called the Liberty Car. Typically, each young woman wore
a sash with the name of a state or territory on it. The position of
highest honor was reserved for Miss Liberty, with Idaho next in
prominence.

47.
*There were at least two
decorated wagons in Idaho
City's parade the year this
was taken. The Luna House is
in the background.*

48.
*This group from the 1890s
featured Mamie Silsby as
Liberty, John Duquette as
Uncle Sam, Sophie Smith as
Idaho, and Mamie Taylor and
Gertrude McDevitt as Peace
and Plenty.*

47

Thanksgiving

Idaho's territorial governors regularly issued a proclamation, often printed in full in the *Idaho World*. But in 1864 Governor Caleb Lyon got around to issuing his only a day before the date already proclaimed by President Abraham Lincoln. The *World* and most other papers missed it. "Idaho, it appears, had nothing to thank God for," complained the editor on December 3. "Gov. Lyon let it slide by without comment, and the people generally knew nothing, and cared nothing about it. Yet if any portion of the Union has cause for Thanksgiving it is Idaho Territory. The states east of the Rocky Mountains can only thank God for the curses of war; we, at least, for the blessings of peace."

This was probably the only time in history that Thanksgiving was not generally observed in Boise Basin towns. In 1865 Governor Lyon's proclamation arrived in time to appear on page one of a *World* supplement on November 18. Following President Andrew Johnson's proclamation of October 28th, Thanksgiving was observed on the first Thursday of December that year. In the flowery language for which Idaho's eccentric governor was noted, Lyon gave thanks "for the garnered grain of our valleys and the gathered gold of our mountains."

This first Thanksgiving after the end of the Civil War was celebrated with a number of special events. A social ball was held on Monday in the Masonic Hall and a "Grand Masquerade Ball" on Wednesday at Oakland Hall on Montgomery street. "Come One, Come All" urged the sponsor's ad, noting that "Tickets can be had in all the principal saloons in the Basin." On Thanksgiving night, "altogether the finest dance of the season," was given. "About forty ladies graced the occasion." Thanksgiving dinners then, as now, were traditional. The *World* referred to "destroying turkeys" as part of the festivities.

In 1880 Rev. E. Hayes conducted a church service Thanksgiving morning, "and in the afternoon fowl made the ordinary sinner feel like offering thanks for the preservation of his appetitive ability," wrote Editor C.E. Jones. "Thanksgiving Day made ready sale this week for chickens, turkeys, ducks, geese and venison," he observed. No church services were held in Idaho City in 1885, but "the people of this place yesterday shuffled off work and vexation of business, rested, rendered Thanks and feasted." In 1886 "Thanksgiving Day was enjoyed by festive and gracious thankers, but was rather rough on Turkey."

Thanksgiving was not always celebrated with religious observances or with social functions in Boise Basin's territorial days, but it was decidedly a special day for families. Single miners sought solace and companionship in the saloons and ate Thanksgiving dinner in one of the restaurants where holiday menus were remarkably varied and complete.

49.
This "fun-loving saloon crowd" was of the kind that enjoyed April Fool tricks in early days.

Other Celebrations

In addition to major holidays, a number of other traditional observances offered the people of Boise Basin opportunities for merry making.

April first, All Fools' Day, was enjoyed annually with pranks that made their targets either laugh or smart. In 1867 "the day was made very lively by the sellers and their victims, all in merry humor together." (A "sell," in the language of the time, was a trick perpetrated on an unsuspecting victim.) "Salted toddies and 'doped' cocktails" were a feature of the day in saloons that year, the doping sometimes taking the form of powerful emetics or laxatives — far from funny to the recipients, and sure to be avenged at the earliest opportunity. In 1870, the fun-loving saloon crowd fired off pistols in the middle of the night, then got Idaho City's lawmen and doctors out of bed to deal with the imaginary battle and carnage.

49

A more innocent prank was that reported in 1885: "The public school bell was silent last Wednesday morning, April 1st. One of the teachers vigorously pulled the rope, but the bell gave forth no sound. A band of boys near the school house whooped and danced like a band of Commanche Indians on the war path. The boys muffled the bell Tuesday night 'to April fool the teachers,' and they succeeded admirably." An 1886 prank was described in less specific terms: "A number of the nimrods of this burg were sent on a wild goose chase yesterday, but got no geese, because there were none, but they got sold. April 1st — all fools day."

Valentines were regularly exchanged, often of the insulting kind known as "penny dreadfuls." Postmaster James A. Pinney, who ran a bookstore in the building now occupied by the Boise Basin Historical Museum, advertised a fresh stock each season. In 1869 romantic and vicious valentines were described as "missives appropriate, if not missiles." Needless to say the "dreadfuls" were sent anonymously, to "conceited fops," ugly spinsters, unpopular teachers, or anyone else upon whom one wished to vent some spleen. Many were unspeakably cruel and must have been hard for their recipients to shrug off.

50.
Schoolboys loved to play pranks on their teachers. This professor probably had his hands full.

51.
Sons of the Emerald Isle joined in annual celebration of St. Patrick's Day. Jerry Riordan was a well known Basin pioneer.

52.
James McDevitt was both a butcher and a miner in 1870. He had a meat market at Placerville in 1890.

53.
John McGonigle edited a number of frontier newspapers, including the Owyhee Avalanche and the Boise News.

50

51

52

53

With a population of over 300 natives of Ireland in 1870, the Basin was naturally the scene of annual observances of St. Patrick's Day. In 1865, for example, the day "was quietly and agreeably commemorated...by the numerous children of the 'Green Isle' in this Basin, and by many others, not to the manor born. The ball at Okanogan Hall, Pioneer City, was attended by many from Centerville and Idaho City, and proved a very cheerful gathering." Next night a continuation of the celebration took place at Centerville in Magnolia Hall.

The Fenian Brotherhood, an Irish-American society dedicated to Irish independence, had an active membership in Boise Basin in the Sixties and early Seventies. Local lodges included the Emmet Circle at Pioneer City, the Sarsfield Circle at Centerville, and the Idaho and Emerald Circles at Idaho City. The Fenians sponsored St. Patrick's balls as social and fund raising events from time to time before the order's demise in 1877. When Idaho City's Emerald Circle was organized in January, 1870, this resolution was adopted:

> That all respectable citizens of Irish, American, or
> European birth or lineage who are kindly disposed to
> the sacred cause which unites us in heart and sentiment,
> are respectfully invited to join our fraternity...

A militant band of 600 Fenians actually invaded Canada in 1866 from upstate New York, for which many of them were eventually arrested and imprisoned. The Boise Basin Fenians contented themselves with sending financial support, passing resolutions, and

54

listening to patriotic speakers. Frank Ganahl, an Idaho City lawyer, was one of the most eloquent orators of his day. A two hour speech he made at a Fenian gathering in Boise City in January, 1867, was described by James O'Meara, Irish-born editor of the *Idaho World* as follows:

"It was, in fact, a classic, historical, beautiful address, well worthy (of) preservation in print as one of the grandest, happiest tributes ever paid by tongue of man to that nation and that people in whose honor, vindication, and cause it was pronounced..." That O'Meara and his fellow Irishmen in the mines of Idaho were moved by love of their homeland is obvious, but then, as now, you didn't have to be Irish to sing "Wearin' of the Green" on St. Patrick's Day.

The Fenian Brotherhood also took the lead in celebrating George Washington's Birthday. The ball held in 1866 in Gymnasium Hall, Idaho City, featured a midnight supper at the Fenian Chop House that "was in excellent taste and gave general satisfaction." The 1869 ball took place in McGregor's Hall. Other February 22nd dances were organized by saloon keepers or proprietors of halls, but in many years there was no observance of the date at all — a fact mentioned with regret by the paper. In 1879 a large crowd from all parts of the Basin traveled over Grimes Pass to Garden Valley for a "grand ball" that lasted until 7 a.m. In winter, when times were dull, people were willing to travel long distances through cold and snow to enjoy themselves at a dance. Once there, they made the most of the opportunity.

May Day was not regularly observed in Boise Basin, but a charming exception took place in 1879 when an outdoor basket social was held to benefit the Sabbath School at Idaho City. "Young gentlemen, you are requested to be present, and inform your ladies to bring your dinner," read the quaintly worded invitation. There is a clear suggestion that the "young gentlemen" were somewhat reluctant to take part in what they may have regarded as an affair for girls and sissies, since the principal events of the day were the braiding of a May pole, with ribbons of red, white and blue, and the crowning of Miss Sadie McClintock as Queen of the May.

Other holidays, only occasionally celebrated through the years, included January 8, anniversary of the Battle of New Orleans in 1815. Jackson Day, as it was usually called, was observed because of the victory and rhetoric of General Andrew Jackson. Placerville saloon keeper Jimmy Hart loved to tell the story of how British General Packenham sent word to the besieged Jackson that he intended to eat his supper in New Orleans. Old Andy replied, according to Jimmy, that "if he did, he would take his breakfast next morning in hell!"

54.
Attorney Frank Ganahl was remembered by a contemporary as "noted for eloquence rather than legal acquirement."

55.
When the Chinese at Centerville celebrated their New Year, the white population turned out too.

The white community in Boise Basin towns could hardly help being aware of Chinese holidays, but understood them not at all. Only when the Orientals celebrated their own New Year festival with fireworks and parties did whites become involved as invited guests. The other Chinese observances were chiefly religious, such as an April, 1870, "feast for the dead" called "Chung Mung." The *World* said, "In accordance with their peculiar religious notions the graveyard opposite town was visited by a large number of Celestials, who took with them plenty of 'grub' for their defunct brethren."

At a festival held in August, 1879, the Chinese "touched off the usual amount of fireworks in the evening," but the paper didn't bother to find out what the occasion was. At some of these observances statues or paintings of gods or ancestors were carried in parades, to the accompaniment of Oriental music that sounded discordant indeed to Western ears. The images reposed in Chinese temples, called "Joss Houses," the rest of the year. ("Joss" is Pidgin English for God, hence a Joss House is God's house, a name Christians also use for their churches).

Cockpits and Dog Fights

Entertainment for Boise Basin miners was often brutal and bloodthirsty by today's standards. "There is to be gay sport at the Pony Saloon tonight," wrote the *Idaho World* on December 3, 1864. "All the dogs in the Territory will be on the rampage, to say nothing of certain belligerent roosters shod for the occasion."

Several Idaho City saloons had "pits" where frenzied mobs of men watched dogs and steel-spurred roosters battle to the death. In January, 1865, "the rival cities of Idaho and Placerville" wagered a stake of $250 on the outcome of a fight between the "representative dogs of the respective towns." Idaho won, and challenged Placerville to a sleigh race for a purse of $1000. The dare was declined, and Idaho crowed.

Admission was usually charged to watch these bloody battles, and the *World* observed that "admirers of that style of pastime" could amuse themselves for the whole evening for 50 cents and wager on each contest as well. All comers were invited to enter their own prize roosters. Matt Zapp, a native of France, built a new cockpit in his Bank Exchange Saloon in January, 1869, and advertised that he had "a fine lot of pure game cocks, imported direct from Europe, ready to be put into the ring...come and see the sport." Zapp sought to undercut Claresey's Saloon, his chief competitor in the field, by offering free admission.

Cock and dog fighting was primarily a winter sport, when most miners had time on their hands and were eager for any novelty or excitement. Although Matt Zapp promoted the fights longer than most, he had new rivals every winter as other saloon keepers tried to hold their customers. Baird & Judge and White & Douglas were among those who offered the blood sports for awhile. Both converted their cockpits back to card rooms after the sport failed to pay.

Dog fights were the more brutal of the two pastimes, and met with more opposition, undoubtedly because men, women and children were attached to pet dogs of their own and hated to see any animal suffer. (It was harder to get sentimental over the fate of roosters, since they were beheaded regularly for the family dinner table.) A typical dog fight ended in the death of the winner as well as the loser. This happened in January, 1869, when a big crowd watched a battle of nearly an hour between John Foy's dog "Bull" and Sam Thompson's "Sank" for $150.

Nineteenth Century Idahoans were especially sensitive to cruelty to horses. Newspaper editors often protested the mistreatment of animals and suggested that the "beasts" who perpetrated such "outrages" ought to be publicly horsewhipped themselves.

If animal fighting and the treatment of animals in those days seems especially barbaric to us, it should be remembered that prize fighting between men was equally brutal. By the rules then in effect

56.
Frontier gamblers dressed like gentlemen. The identity of this early resident of Boise Basin has been lost.

57.
Dan Mulford was one of the gambling fraternity who made his living "mining miners."

(although the sport was outlawed in most places) a "round" was not over until one of the bare-fisted pugilists had been knocked down. In the celebrated 1889 bareknuckle championship fight between John L. Sullivan and Jake Kilrain the two knocked each other down 75 times.

Soiled Doves

Mining camps in the West attracted their share of prostitutes, gamblers, thieves, and confidence men as soon as there were enough people there to make it profitable. "Mining miners" was the occupation of a substantial number of individuals in all districts, and Boise Basin was no exception.

The compilers of the 1870 census explained that it was difficult to know how many such people there were, since most men and women in disreputable occupations did not admit to them, or disguised them "under ambiguous terms," such as "boarding house keepers," when they were really keepers of brothels. The census did not omit tabulation of these occupations out of feelings of delicacy, it was pointed out, or out of unwillingness to admit that there were such people in most communities, but only because accurate data could not be obtained. In rare cases, the compiler explained, "such persons had the assurance to report themselves by their true designations, or assistant marshals took the responsibility (and sometimes the risk) of writing down the real occupations of these classes..."

The marshals in charge of the Boise county census of 1870 "took the risk," and did record nine prostitutes: three in Idaho City, two in Placerville and one in Pioneerville. One woman lived with a gambler and another with a well known saloon keeper of Idaho City. That there were numerous other "soiled doves" in the Basin is certain, as occasional references to "the demi-monde" in the *Idaho World* make clear. The brutal 1870 murder of a Mexican packer in Idaho City, for example, took place in "a house of ill fame kept by a woman sailing under the sobriquet of 'The Rocky Mountain son of a bitch,' apparently a very appropriate name in consonance with the character of the possessor." The man had been horribly beaten and dumped into a stream of water running down the street outside her house.

An 1866 account quaintly describes two Idaho City prostitutes as "a couple of nymphs, not having the fear of God nor respect of men very high." They were brought before a judge "charged with profaning the atmosphere with loud and obscene language." One was fined $50, the other $5, and they were sent on their way "with the injunction to keep the peace hereafter."

Quartzburg's red light district produced a riot in 1871. "Nobody killed," reported the paper, "though considerable whisky disposed of." A few months later in that town "a woman of the demi-monde, known as Kitty King, committed suicide by taking an overdose of morphine." Behind items like this, we sense the personal tragedies of such women in Basin camps. Their daily lives were degrading, they were despised by "decent women" in the towns, and suffered low self-esteem as well. For most, the future was bleak and uncertain. Not surprisingly, they drank heavily, often turned to drugs, and sank lower and lower until suicide seemed the only way out of a wretched existence. Venereal disease and abortion, under primitive conditions of treatment, also took their toll, making the life expectancy of a fallen woman short.

For Chinese prostitutes it was even worse. Many were brought to America as slaves, having been sold as young girls by their destitute peasant parents. They might pass through several hands before ending up in mining camps like those of the Basin. Suicides and attempted suicides of such unfortunate women were not uncommon. The *World* reported one such case in 1879 and was indignant about it:

"A Chinawoman came up from Boise City a few days ago, and being pursued by her owner, took poison in preference to being taken back. Dr. Zipf was called and saved her life. The brutal treatment of the owners of Chinese women has caused two or three to attempt suicide within the last two or three months. The women are beginning to find out, however, that slavery is not recognized by the laws of this country, and some of them refuse to be treated as slaves. An example ought to be made of some of the brutes."

A Chinese girl, called by the *Idaho Tri-weekly Statesman*, "the most beautiful maiden in all Canton," was spared the fate of her sisters in 1875, thanks to a court case. "The beautiful Annie Lee" came to America with a supposed friend to look for her childhood sweetheart, Ah Guan. Once in Idaho City, however, the friend "claimed her as his property, and proposed to sell her into prostitution." She was able to find her sweetheart and to flee to Boise City, where Territorial Secretary Curtis married them. The Yen Wah Co. of Idaho City, which had so nearly secured Annie, and "still coveted the fair maiden as their common property," procured a warrant for her arrest, charging her with grand larceny when she left Idaho City. (The treasure she had stolen from the Yen Wahs was quite obviously herself.) When she was finally found and taken back to Idaho City, Boise's See Yup Co. came to the aid of her husband by hiring an able attorney. He secured a writ of habeas corpus to bring her back to Boise City, but doing so was a touchy task, since Idaho City's Chinese were now anxious to keep her. Nearly 500 of them gathered "just in time to see their bird fly away."

58.
Merchant Lo Kee of Idaho City with his wife and son. Chinese families were rare in the Basin in the 1860s.

Before a large courtroom crowd in Boise, about half of it Chinese, Judge Clark asked Annie if she wanted to go back to Idaho City or stay in Boise. She emphatically chose Boise. Asked if they had made her stay in Idaho City, she said "Yes." "Who?" "All Chinamen there," she said. She loved her man and wanted to go with him. The judge told her she was free to go with anyone she wanted to, at which her attorney placed her arm in that of Ah Guan, her husband, and the two of them marched out of the court house "with no little merriment for the court and by-standers."

A few Chinese women in Idaho were married to merchants and professional men, but Thomas Donaldson estimated that of about 4000 Chinese in the Territory in the 1870s, only about 75 were women, "of whom the great majority were making a living by immoral ways; the distinction should be made, however, that they were for the convenience of their own countrymen."

58

Germans

59

The Germans played a prominent role in the life of Boise Basin's mining communities. Only the Chinese and the Irish outnumbered them among the foreign born. Although the majority worked as miners, a significant number were merchants or followed a trade. Prussian-born Herman Zipf was a leading physician and surgeon. There were, not surprisingly, many brewers, some saloon keepers, several butchers and shoemakers. A number of the clothing and dry goods merchants were German Jews. The Germans had a sense of national identity through a common language and cultural traditions, even though there was no German union until after the Franco-Prussian War of 1870. Instead, Boise Basin's Germans said they were from Saxony, Bavaria, Hesse, Prussia, Wurttemberg, or one of a dozen other small German states.

Idaho City had a German Literary Club in 1869, but more notable was the part Germans had played in the community's musical life. The Idaho City Brass Band, at one time or another, was made up entirely of Germans, and was often referred to simply as the German Band. Adolf Ballot, a watchmaker and jeweler, was active in Idaho City musical ensembles before moving to Boise City in the mid-eighties where he helped organize the Boise Philharmonic Orchestra.

News of the Franco-Prussian War had an immediate impact on Germans on the Idaho frontier. Nearly all had family and friends in "the Fatherland" and since France was conceded by the experts to have "the finest and most powerful fighting machine in the world," there were grave fears for the folks back home. The war pulled Germans together as nothing had before, and they had the support and sympathy of most other Idahoans. Napoleon III, Emperor of the French, was regarded as the greatest threat to European peace and stability since the defeat and exile of his uncle, Napoleon Bonaparte, in 1815.

One of the first organized actions of Idaho's Germans was to start a relief fund for the aid of wounded soldiers and the widows and orphans of men killed in the fighting. At Idaho City a committee composed of S.G. Rosenbaum, Charles Bernstiel and Charles Lautenschlager published an appeal in the *Idaho World* which drew immediate and generous response. Bernstiel was a popular young merchant from Bavaria, Lautenschlager was a Hessian brewer, and Rosenbaum a retired merchant of German-Swiss origin.

Charley Bernstiel was a leader in arousing patriotic feelings among his countrymen. He traveled back and forth between the Basin and Boise City making speeches and encouraging support. When the incredible news came in early September, 1870, that the French had suffered a crushing defeat at Sedan, where Napoleon III had been surrounded and captured, Bernstiel led the rejoicing. Calling him a "true blue Prussian," *Idaho World* editor George Ainslie acknowledged Bernstiel's gift of a case of champagne to the newspaper office to celebrate the German victory.

59.
Dr. Herman Zipf, a graduate of the University of Heidelberg, started his Idaho City practice in 1868. He died in 1900.

60.
Isidore Smith was one of several well known German merchants of Idaho City.

61.
Beer was cheap in Idaho City in 1867.

French miners and sympathizers were stunned. They could not believe the news and refused to accept it. Some were rash enough to bet large sums of money, and even their gold watches, that it was all an unfounded rumor. When the news was verified as all too true the German celebrations resumed with added gusto. Some were still going on months later.

On one of his return trips to Idaho City from Boise, Charley Bernstiel decorated the horses on the Idaho City stage with little Prussian flags. "He is bound to vent his enthusiasm in some way," observed the newspaper. A week later the young merchant, who had sold his business, was on his way home to the Fatherland. The war had ended so fast that no Idaho Germans got home in time to enlist in the army, but one man tried.

"Off for the War," noted the *World.* Our Teutonic friend Louis Reid, of the Miner's Brewery, caught the war fever and started a few days ago for the Fatherland to join the Prussian Army. He takes with him the best wishes of his friends who hope to see him return here safe and sound when the war closes." None would see him alive again, for the unfortunate man went insane before he reached the railroad. He jumped off the stage coach several times and finally wandered off and died before a search party could find him.

Nearly all the breweries in Boise Basin were run by Germans. In 1864 Joseph Helmuth and H.C. Wiebold ran the Boise Brewery at Placerville, Pioneerville's German bewers were C. Bornhaeuser, L. Haubrich, H. Inkamp, C. Laudenslayer, and A. Schlumb.

Other German-born residents of the Basin made unique contributions to the character of mining city life. Few were better known than the dance hall girls called "Hurdy-Gurdies."

Hurdy-Gurdy Girls

An institution in most Western mining camps of the 1860s was the hurdy-gurdy house. Although some regarded the women employed in them as little better than prostitutes, old-timers of the Basin rose to their defense, both in the Sixties and in later reminiscences. When James S. Reynolds, editor of the *Idaho Tri-weekly Statesman* urged the 1864 legislature to tax the hurdy-gurdy girls "because they are Swiss, chubby, black, can't talk English, and live in the rear of the dance house on the cheapest kind of plunder," H.C. Street, editor of the *Idaho World,* replied that Reynolds was being malicious because he had, "from appearances, been sacked by some hurdy-gurdy." Street said he had never seen a black hurdy in the Territory, that they were from Germany, and were the same color as Reynolds. "Hundreds of our citizens, whose fathers and mothers are waiting for their wandering sons and daughters to returns to the sunny banks of the Oder, the Elbe, and the Rhine, do not feel very highly complimented by the *Statesman's* slurs on their complexion."

Former Governor and U.S. Senator William J. McConnell, in his *Early History of Idaho*, also defended the hurdies. McConnell, who was in the Basin in the 1860s, described what a hurdy-gurdy house really was:

"Saloons were more numerous in all mining towns than any other class of business, and as gambling was usually an adjunct, every effort possible was made to make them attractive. Talented musicians were employed at high salaries, and not infrequently girls, called 'hurdy-gurdies,' were engaged to dance with all comers who desired that kind of amusement at the nominal price of fifty cents per dance, and the drinks for self and partner, which cost fifty cents more, or one dollar net per dance.

"The girls were engaged by the proprietors of the 'social resorts,' in sets of four, with a chaperone, who accompanied them at all times.

"They were almost invariably German girls, and although they were brought into contact with rough people and sometimes witnessed even the shedding of human blood, the rude, generous chivalry of the mountain men, some of whom were always found in these resorts, was a guarantee of protection from violence, and strange as it may sound to those of modern times, these girls were pure women, who simply did the work they had bargained to do...
The poor girls, and they danced only because they were poor, had kind hearts and wonderful patience and forbearance."

The 1870 census listed one "hurdy-gurdy troop" in Boise Basin, at Granite Creek. Although most of the hurdies had left the mining camps by that time, the makeup of this one, living at one address, is probably typical. Conrad Schneider, violinist, and his wife Catherine, natives of Hesse-Darmstadt, Germany, lived with their three children in a saloon and rooming house run by James Mathews. The company included two other male violinists, and four dancing girls, aged 15, 17, 18 and 27. All were from Hesse or Prussia.

According to McConnell, many of these young women saved their money, retired from dancing, married miners, raised families and lived out their lives in Boise Basin.

Johnny Kelly

No musician who ever visited the mining camps of Idaho and the West was better known or more universally admired than Johnny Kelly. Kelly's ability to move an audience of rough old miners to tears with his violin playing was legendary. "As an artist with the bow he had no equal in that day," recalled former Governor William McConnell. "He could make his pet instrument tell a plaintive tale of home and mother, or of tearful ones who awaited, oft in vain, the return of father, brother or lover; again he would arouse the reckless instincts of his hearers by some rolicking tune which told of wine and song."

62.
Idaho City had a Miners' Exchange saloon from as early as 1864. One of its descendents in the same location was Melvin Weigel's place.

58

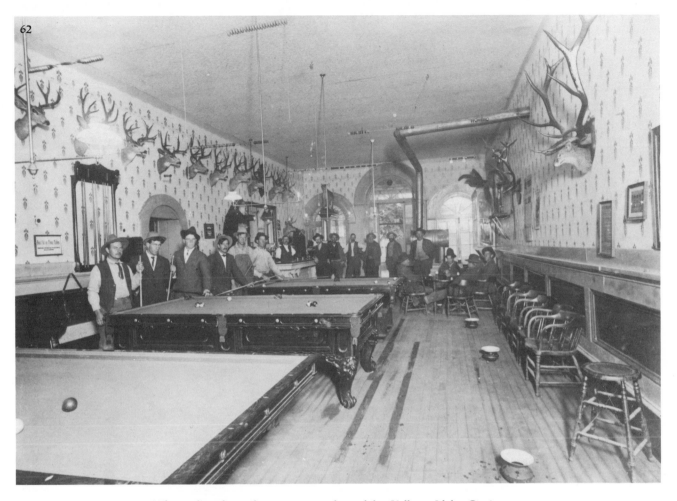

When a benefit performance was planned for Kelly at Idaho City's Forrest Theater in February, 1865, the *Idaho World* urged its readers to fill the house. "Mr. Kelly is one of the pioneer dramatists of this territory, and has done much to furnish the public with the means of whiling away the tedious hours." The "tedious hours" referred to were the long days and nights of winter when miners were idle and thoughts of home and loved ones could not be crowded out by hard work or hard drink.

Since Kelly was Irish, he had an especial appeal to Boise Basin's large Irish population — most numerous national group in the mines until the Chinese influx of the late Sixties. McConnell called Kelly "a big-hearted son of the Emerald Isle," and recalled that he often, through "untoward circumstances," had to ply his trade in gambling

houses and saloons rather than theaters or concert halls.
McConnell's description of Kelly in action in an Idaho City "den of
iniquity" is the best we have:

63.
Idaho City's brass band posed
in splendid new uniforms for
this early-day picture. The
town was rarely without a
band of some kind.

> He commanded a salary second to none and was
> engaged in the largest gambling resort in the city. The
> contract under which he played included the installation
> of a swinging stage or platform, swung by iron rods
> from the upper joists, several feet above the heads of
> those who might stand on the main floor below. This
> platform was reached by a movable ladder, which, after
> he ascended, he pulled up out of reach of those below.
> The object was two-fold; first, when located upon his
> aerie, he was removed from the danger of panics which
> were an almost nightly occurrence, caused from the
> sportive instincts of some visitor who, having imbibed
> too freely of the regulation vest-pocket whiskey, or
> having suffered some real or imaginary grievance,
> proceeded to distibute the leaden pellets of a Colt's navy
> revolver, not only into the anatomy of the offender, but
> quite as frequently to the serious, if not fatal injury of
> some innocent bystander.
>
> When it is understood that it was not unusual for 500
> men to be present in the room at the time these
> diversions occurred, it is not difficult to imagine the
> kind of panic liable to ensue. Hence the first object of
> Kelly's lofty perch. His second object was to be above
> the course of flying missiles and thus preserve his violin,
> which was a valuable one, from the chance of being
> perforated by stray bullets.

Fine musician that he was, Kelly had to present enough variety in
his programs to hold the attention of his boisterous audiences. An
Idaho Tri-weekly Statesman item of August 26, 1865, describes the
format. "John Kelly, the musician and vocalist, with his wonderful
Indian, arrived in this city yesterday, and will give one of his grand
parlor entertainments this evening."

"His wonderful Indian" was Willie, a Shoshoni lad who had been
captured when his family was killed by a party of white raiders.
He was given to Kelly, who raised him and taught him to play the
violin. The Indian boy showed remarkable talent as a showman,
and was especially adept at acrobatics and contortionist tricks.
Johnny Kelly and wonderful Willie traveled all over the United
States and even to Ireland when Kelly visited his old home in the
1870s. It was there that Willie died.

Bands

Idaho City and other Boise Basin mining towns had brass bands of their own at an early date, made up of local men who had learned to play an instrument sometime before following the gold rush to Idaho. That they added a great deal to the life and spirit of the mining frontier is evidenced by the frequency with which they are mentioned in early newspapers.

"The Idaho Band has become one of the most attractive fixtures of the city," said the *Idaho World* in November, 1864. "Through the Summer and during the Fall campaign, it kept the political parties marching to the sound of its martial airs. The piping times of peace having succeeded the stormy era of politics, the Band adjusts itself to the spirit of the times." The Idaho City band of 1864 was a modest aggregation of only five members, but later groups were considerably larger.

Placerville had a brass band with a dozen members as early as February, 1865, when a benefit musical was held for the Christian Sanitary Organization of that town. $200 for medical supplies was raised to be sent East to aid Civil War wounded. From the *World's* comment that "not a word was said to mar the harmony and pleasure of those present," it seems likely that Southern as well as Union sympathizers were in the Placerville crowd that day, and that the fund was for the relief of soldiers on both sides. The long and bloody war between the states was nearing its close at the time. Boise Basin had more Southerners than Northerners.

Two weeks later, the Placerville Brass Band came to Idaho City and serenaded the office of the *Idaho World*. Editor H.C. Street thanked them for the compliment, noting that their melodies took the keenness out of the frosty air, "and falling from the hill over the snow, enveloped town as gently as 'a summer's cloud."

Serenading a newspaper editor was a sure way for a band to get attention in the columns of his paper. James O'Meara was editor of the *World* in 1869 when the Idaho City band played outside his house. "Their music was excellent," wrote O'Meara, "and their selections, vocal and instrumental, were happily made and charmingly executed." In 1870 Centerville's brass band came to Idaho City and joined the local organization to serenade the town. New Editor George Ainslie returned thanks for the combined effort this time, calling it "a musical treat" and "some of the best music we have ever heard in the Territory."

A May, 1870 serenade was offered by "the German Brass Band" of Idaho City. It played throughout the town from about 10 p.m. until 4 in the morning. "If the musicians and friends accompanying omitted any citizens in the city we have not heard of it," commented Ainslie. Far from being put out by the loss of sleep such serenading must have caused, the Idahoans loved it. "Do some more, gents, 'ef you please," wrote the editor.

By 1879 there was no longer a band in Idaho City and the paper asked why one couldn't be organized, since there were a good many amateur musicians in town. Soon after, Professor Gilbert Butler arrived from Silver City to take over Idaho City's public school. One of the energetic and talented professor's first acts was to start a boys' band. After a few weeks of practice, the boys ventured to play some tunes in the street. The *World* was encouraging, and thought it "pretty good music" for such a young organization.

64.
Charles Ostner studied art in Heidelberg.

65.
This is Ostner's own painting of the presentation of his Washington *in Boise City, January 8, 1869.*

66.
Ostner's George Washington *as it looks today in Idaho's capitol building.*

67.
Orlando "Rube" Robbins, famed Indian fighter and frontier lawman was the inspiration for Ostner's The Scout.

64

65

66

67

Charles Ostner

One of the most interesting and talented German pioneers of Boise County was Charles Ostner. Although he followed the lure of mining all his life, it was Ostner's artistic ability that brought him local fame, if not fortune.

In February, 1865, Ostner ran a notice in the *Idaho World* stating his intention of building a toll road from Placerville to Thomas' ranch on the Payette river in Garden Valley — a distance of about 12 miles — and of asking the county commissioners at their April meeting for a license to operate it. This was granted.

On February 22, 1865, according to an account he gave later, Ostner cut down a large Ponderosa pine tree. In his spare time he began carving a nearly life-size statue of George Washington on horseback. Tradition says that he often carved at night by the light of a torch held by one of his children, and that he took the likeness of Washington from a postage stamp. By the time the statue was finished in 1868, word of it had spread around the Basin and many were curious to see it. Ostner therefore placed an ad in the *World* announcing that his "splended and curious work of art" would be shown in Centerville on Christmas Day, and in Idaho City two days later. It would then be taken to Boise and given to the people of Idaho for permanent display there. The ad called it "the only work of its kind on the Pacific coast," and urged people to come see it (for one dollar).

The *World* described it as "Ostner's famous equestrian statue...the result of his own ingenious labor...." The carving was presented to Governor David Ballard and other officials at Boise City on January 8, 1869, "in the midst of a blinding snow storm." It was dedicated to the pioneers of Idaho. Ostner himself painted a picture of the occasion. He settled in Boise thereafter and tried to support himself by his art. Forced to try his hand at whatever came along in this line, he carved tombstones, designed buildings, and drew views of Boise City and other Idaho towns, some of which were lithographed in San Francisco and sold by subscription. A few of his oil paintings survive, including his equestrian of Orlando "Rube" Robbins called *The Scout*. His *Washington*, in the Idaho capitol, is considered one of state's treasures.

Fire! Fire!

"Idaho City in Ashes" proclaimed the headline. "The whole town was consumed from Bear Run to Commercial street, which is nearly to the foot of Main, and from the bluff to More's creek," reported the *Idaho Tri-weekly Statesman* on May 20, 1865. Idaho City's great fire of May 18, 1865, lighted the sky with a blaze and column of smoke that could be seen clearly in Boise City 30 miles away.

"Not a single hotel was left in Idaho City on the morning after the fire...Several extempore tables were put up in the gulches, and many were fed at private houses," said the *Idaho World*. What survived was a livery stable, one store, the Catholic church, the Methodist church, the Jenny Lind Theater, and the *Idaho World* office. A "few shanties" on the outskirts of town also escaped. Father Poulin opened his church to hospital patients and "the theater and newspaper office were crowded with families and the homeless generally."

Although every saloon in town was destroyed, there was plenty of liquor in circulation. The reaction of a great many that fateful night was to grab everything they could and run with it. "Persons who were present...think that a class of men called 'honest miners' of that locality can outsteal any set of men outside Botany Bay." Within a week over $10,000 worth of stolen property had been recovered, but placer miners were still uncovering caches of goods years later — most of it decayed and worthless by then.

Rebuilding began at once. A week after the disaster "a line of buildings is already seen along the whole length of Main street, many of them being built in a more substantial manner than before." Although most people lost everything they had, a few merchants with fireproof cellars still had goods to sell, and were back in business within days. *The Statesman* thought Idaho City's recovery "magical," and said that new hotels larger and better than those destroyed were already under construction. "Many of the substantial miners advanced business men idle dust to enable them to build and start again."

An eye witness, writing eight days after the blaze, said the fire had started in a hurdy-gurdy house on Montgomery street at 9:30 p.m. An hour and a half later the town was gone. The Jenny Lind Theater, one of the few surviving structures, was playing "Colleen Bawn" to packed houses every night. Stolen goods were still being found in the woods, and building was proceeding as fast as possible. If the lumber were available, the writer thought, the town would already be rebuilt, better than before.

Although Idaho City had often been warned of the danger of a fire catastrophe, no regular fire department had been organized. Probably a volunteer organization, no matter how efficient, would have been helpless under the circumstances. A strong wind was blowing and the ramshackle wooden buildings, packed tightly together, were ablaze before men with hooks and axes could react.

68.
Idaho City's merchants advertised proudly that they were back in business only days after the 1867 fire.

It is doubtful that the best modern equipment could have saved much once the fire was well underway.

In April, 1867, Idaho Hook & Ladder Co. No. 1 was organized, and on May 11, 1867, the *World* noted that the company was just completing a building for its wagons, ladders, hose and buckets. On May 17, 1867, as *World* editor James O'Meara was just finishing an article noting that the following day would be the second anniversary of the great fire of May 18, 1865, he heard the fateful cry of "fire! fire!" once more. Within minutes general panic had set in as wind-driven flames made efforts to save the buildings impossible. In less than three hours Idaho City was once again in ashes, with losses estimated at more than a million dollars. 440 buildings were destroyed, more than half of them businesses.

Great forest fires were of regular occurrence in Boise Basin, and there was nothing to be done but let them run their course. Isolated miners' cabins and placer flumes were occasionally destroyed. In 1870 the forest was ablaze in all directions around Idaho City, extending all the way north and west to the Payette river. People suffered greatly from mosquitoes, since smoke in the woods seemed to drive them into town. A series of lightning caused fires in 1879 raised concern over "the beautiful timber southeast of town" that was being destroyed. This fire burned through the Thorn creek area in a belt several miles wide — scene of a similar burn nearly a century later. These 1879 fires burned almost continuously from mid-July until the first of October when rains finally put them out.

Placerville was nearly wiped out by fire in September, 1874, but quickly rebuilt. On August 17, 1899, the little town was again struck by a disastrous blaze that left only 14 houses, the school, and about half the Chinese neighborhood. Given the flimsy wooden buildings and lack of firefighting equipment of those days, it was a lucky town indeed that did not sooner or later have a major conflagration.

69.
Centerville sent wagonloads of supplies to the relief of Placerville fire victims in 1899.

70.
The Idaho City brass band helped Placerville celebrate an early-day Fourth of July.

71.
Placerville is laid out like a California town, around a central plaza. This lithograph shows what it looked like in the early 1880s.

69

70

71

ELLIOTT.LITH. 421 MONT.ST.

Bogus Gold

Gold dust, rather than coin or currency, was the usual medium of exchange in the 1860s in Boise Basin. This created a number of problems. In the first place, all gold found in its natural state contains some silver, commonly from 5 to 20 percent. Since gold was usually rated at 16 times the value of silver, gold dust from different parts of the Basin could vary greatly in worth. Without assaying, there was no way to know for sure the value of any particular dust offered in trade. Since assaying is a complex process, it obviously was not practical to test all of the gold dust that changed hands every day.

A more serious factor affecting the value of gold dust was deliberate adulteration or counterfeiting. Filings of brass, lead, or other base metals were added to genuine gold dust or given a thin coating of gold to look like the real thing. If a merchant had reason to suspect he was being offered bogus dust, a simple acid test could be applied. Real gold resisted the acid, base metals dissolved in it — hence the term still in common usage of applying "the acid test" to something of doubtful value or feasibility.

When a tin box containing what looked like two or three hundred dollars worth of gold dust was discovered under the floorboards of Idaho City's Forrest Theater in February, 1865, the test was applied and the acid rapidly consumed the whole package. It was theorized that some crook had hidden the bogus dust at a time when he feared imminent apprehension and didn't want the damning evidence found on his person. Although the acid test was considerably simpler than assaying, it wasn't practical to apply it to every transaction, either.

As the amount of adulterated gold dust in circulation increased, merchants raised prices to offset its progressive loss of value. They also held meetings to discuss the problem and passed resolutions, like that adopted at Centerville in 1867, refusing "the dust used as a circulating medium in Idaho City at any price." Since they did agree to continue acceptance of dust "from the mines of Centerville, Placerville, Pioneer, Applejack, Muddy, and Boston, at the usual rates, until we have a more convenient method of testing its real value, or a different circulating medium," they apparently felt that Idaho City's dust was considerably more debased than their own.

A new bogus dust was discovered in 1869 that was not affected by cold acid, but when boiling acid was applied "after some minutes there bubbles up a thick scum, the color of blood, as thick as molasses." Even the old tried and true acid test could be beaten by some determined counterfeiters, it seems.

When a cache of brass dust was discovered on the site of "the store of Parks & Jenks, noted bogus dust and spurious green-back operators," in July, 1869, the *World* took some satisfaction in telling its readers that the two had been "hung by Vigilantes in 1865, on Snake river, while on their way from this Basin to Montana..."

Paul Buzzini's hydraulic placer operation was pictured in Elliott's 1884 history.

PAUL BUZZINI & CO'S MINE, MOORE CREEK, 4 MILES FROM IDAHO CITY, IDAHO.

The Idaho Territorial Legislature recognized the seriousness of the crime by an act of December 31, 1864, establishing a prison term of not less than 15 years for anyone convicted of manufacturing, selling, or trading in counterfeit gold, but most counterfeiters got off a lot easier than that. A Chinese named Ah Yet, convicted of passing bogus dust in 1870, for example, was sentenced to one year. Had there been evidence to prove that he had manufactured the dust rather than simply passed it, he might have fared worse.

Counterfeiting and manipulation of gold dust of varying values was so common in the 1860s that convictions were hard to obtain. "The editor of the *Owyhee Avalanche* facetiously commented that some individuals were acquitted on the grounds that what they had counterfeited was better than what was in general use."

The extent of this kind of crime in Idaho was further revealed in 1879 when "a party from Bonanza discovered an old cabin on Loon creek that must once have been quite an extensive counterfeiting establishment. In a room beneath the floor were crucibles, moulds, metal and everything necessary for successfully carrying on the manufacture of counterfeit coin..." This *Idaho World* account, headed "Counterfeiters' Roost," recalls another such site near the western edge of Boise Basin. The name Bogus Basin survives from the days when counterfeiting was all too common in Idaho's mining regions.

George Ainslie

George Ainslie arrived in Idaho City on July 6, 1863, and opened a law office at Centerville in 1864. The active role he took in Democratic politics led to his election to the Territorial Legislature in December, 1866. Despite the fact that at 28 he was its youngest member, the Legislative Council chose him as president. His political skill and personal charm had already marked him for leadership.

In September, 1869, Ainslie became editor of the *Idaho World*, Democratic arch-rival of the Republican *Idaho Tri-weekly Statesman* of Boise. When he took over there was a well-established tradition of outrageous slander and insult between the two papers, made more emotional by the Civil War. The *World* spoke for the Basin's dominant Southern and Irish population. The *Statesman* was Radical Republican in its positions.

It is a mark of George Ainslie's political skill and versatility that he could not only take over editorship of a newspaper with no prior journalistic experience, but that he could win the respect and liking of his editorial rival and other Republicans as well.

James O'Meara, Ainslie's predecessor at the *World*, had been thoroughly detested by James Reynolds, editor of the *Statesman*, who once characterized him as a "sickly half-crazed object of pity" who disregarded "all sense of honor, manhood and decency in conducting his paper." O'Meara, not to be outdone, called Reynolds "a consummate ass," and spoke of "the poisonous miasma of (his) fetid body" and "putrescent volume exhaled from (his) nasty mouth."

What a contrast, then, is the editorial reign of George Ainslie. Within a few weeks he is referring to "our dear friend Reynolds of the *Statesman*," and praising the generosity of his editorial colleague for bringing a load of fresh Baltimore oysters to Idaho City and sharing them. "Jim knows what's nice, and he doesn't forget his friends when he has a good thing."

Politically, Reynolds and Ainslie saw eye-to-eye on one thing. They wanted Idaho men appointed to territorial office — not carpet-baggers. "If we are to be damned with Radical officials," wrote Ainslie, "we certainly prefer Idaho Radicals to any of the imported stock." In February, 1870, Ainslie praised the U.S. Senate's confirmation of E.J. Curtis as Territorial Secretary, saying "he has given universal satisfaction, and although he is a Radical he believes a man can be a Democrat and yet be an honest man and a gentleman."

Thomas Donaldson, a leading Republican lawyer who came to Idaho to hold a series of appointive positions, recalled George Ainslie in his memoirs as "too much of a politician to be a strong lawyer, but had he stuck to law none could have excelled him." In 1878 Ainslie was elected to the first of two terms as Idaho's delegate

73.
George Ainslie was a significant figure in Boise Basin's early history, as lawyer, politician, and editor of the Idaho World.

74.
This World *office was one of several locations where the Basin's pioneer newspaper was published between 1864 and 1918.*

in Congress. Donaldson recalled that "during his service at Washington I saw much of him and always respected him despite his bitter political views."

Ainslie "won the good will of the Republicans as well as the Democrats," said Donaldson, because he succeeded in getting everything for Idaho that a territorial delegate could possibly achieve. Describing an interview with President Hayes that he had arranged for Ainslie, Donaldson called the Democrat's presentation "suave and adroit" and "cleverly done in a very few words." On that occasion, too, George Ainslie got what he wanted for Idaho.

Churches

Church services were held in the new Boise Basin towns starting in 1863. Father Toussaint Mesplie was sent to minister to the Catholic population in June and Father Andre Poulin joined him in September. In addition to the large Irish population in the mines there were French, German and Portugese Catholics. Father Mesplie was a genial and popular priest who had already been on the frontier for many years working among the Indians before being sent to Idaho. Mesplie was resident priest at Placerville, Father Poulin at Idaho City.

St. Joseph's Catholic Church was built in Idaho City in time for services in November, 1863; St. Thomas' Church at Placerville, and St. Dominic's Church at Centerville were both dedicated in December, 1863, and St. Francis' Church in Pioneerville in September, 1864.

Protestant services held in Idaho CIty in 1864 were advertised as "open to all denominations." The earliest regular ministers were a Baptist, Reverend Hamilton, and C.S. Kingsley, a Methodist. C.H.E. Newton, of the Methodist Episcopal Church South, arrived from Oregon in December. (The Southern Methodists had split off from the main body over the slavery issue in 1845). William Roberts was another early Protestant preacher in the Basin.

Episcopal Bishop Daniel J. Tuttle made a strong impression on early residents, and was remembered long after for his powerful physique, open and hearty manner, and speaking ability. When he preached in the courthouse in Idaho City in October, 1869, George Ainslie called it "one of the finest sermons we have listened to for many years," and hoped that the Bishop could be induced to settle in the city permanently. G.D.B. Miller, Episcopal rector in Boise City, visited the Basin regularly thereafter, leading Ainslie to comment "a little church service won't hurt a mining community much."

The 1870 Census recorded but two active organizations in Boise County — Episcopal and Catholic. Only the Catholics had a church building at the time — St. Joseph's in Idaho City, rebuilt after the 1867 fire destroyed the first structure. Earlier Protestant churches lost in the fires of 1865 and 1867 had not been rebuilt, but services by both Episcopalians and Methodists were held fairly regularly in the courthouse. Reverend I.D. Driver of the American Bible Society visited in July, 1870. "As he had the reputation of being a 'nail driving' preacher," said the *World*, "he will doubtless have a good congregation present to hear him." Good preaching drew crowds in the 1870s. The Methodists held revival meetings at which R.R. Jones of Ohio, and J. McKeen, Presiding Elder, preached fiery sermons that garnered 22 new members in two weeks. Of a Bishop Tuttle visit, the *World* said, "His eloquence generally stirs up what little religious sentiment there is in any mining community," and after Episcopal Reverend Bollard preached "a very eloquent and impressive sermon" at Centerville in 1879, the paper said

75.
Episcopal Bishop Daniel Sylvester Tuttle impressed all who knew him on the Idaho Frontier. He often preached in Boise Basin towns.

76.
Popular Father Toussaint Mesplie ministered to Roman Catholic miners for a generation. He arrived in June, 1863.

77.
St. Joseph's Catholic church was rebuilt after Idaho City's big 1867 fire. It still stands in modest dignity on East Hill.

75

76

"to ascertain just how a minister stands in the estimation of ye old miner here, one must drop into Chris Meffert's saloon after service." Comments picked up on that occasion were, "He's my man," "Bully preacher, that — like the man first rate, but don't like his white shirt; it's too durned long." What the editor liked best was Bollard's clear delivery: "For the word God he says God, not gawd or gourde..." When Roman Catholic Bishop Glorieux visited the Basin in the Eighties the paper praised his "easy, graceful delivery," and said that he had "a natural gift as an orator."

Jewish holy days were observed faithfully by "our citizens of Hebrew origin," according to the *World*, and were usually mentioned in the paper's columns.

Pinkham — Patterson

On Sunday evening, July 23, 1865, former Boise County Sheriff Sumner Pinkham was shot and killed by Ferdinand Patterson at the Warm Springs resort near Idaho City. Although shooting deaths were relatively commonplace in the mining camps of Idaho at the time, this one had political overtones that aroused powerful emotion and fiery rhetoric.

After Idaho Territory had been established in 1863, in the midst of the Civil War, and before a system for electing local officials had been set up, President Abraham Lincoln appointed Judges for three judicial districts and a United States Marshal for Idaho. Sheriffs were appointed for each of the counties. Naturally, only loyal Republicans and Union sympathizers received these appointments.

When the first county elections were held, the large population of Southerners in the mining camps, augmented by recent Irish immigrants, overwhelmingly voted Democratic. This created the dangerous system of Republican judges and marshals, loyal to the federal government and the northern cause, attempting to maintain law and order and administer justice, when local law enforcement and justice was controlled by Democrats with Southern sympathies.

Sumner Pinkham, a Republican, was Boise County's appointed sheriff. He served only until his successor, a Democrat, was elected. William J. McConnell, who organized Payette Valley vigilantes in 1863, and helped form Boise and Idaho City groups later, recalled the ex-sheriff as "one of Nature's noblemen, six feet two inches tall, with the frame of an athlete...not only physically, but mentally, he was a leader among men...marked from the first for the bullet of an assassin."

McConnell, a life-long Republican, later Governor and U.S. Senator, maintained that the formation of vigilante committees had been justified because elected officials refused to bring criminals to justice. His account of the showdown that resulted in the death of Pinkham, written many years later, is an emotional and biased one. In contrast to his admiring description of Marshal Pinkham is his characterization of Ferdinand J. Patterson as a gambler who had murdered in cold blood the captain of a ship in Portland "in revenge for an imaginary insult," and then had scalped his mistress with a Bowie knife.

James S. Reynolds, editor of the Radical Republican *Idaho Tri-Weekly Statesman*, and one of the leaders of the Boise vigilantes, screamed for Patterson's blood. Not surprisingly, given the spirit of the times, the Democrat *Idaho World* took an entirely different view, consistently supporting local officials and decrying vigilante justice. Editor H.C. Street asked sarcastically "why someone does not abolish all the Courts and all the Juries of the Territory and appoint the editor of the Statesman to perform their functions? It would be much cheaper and more expeditious, for he

78.
Sumner Pinkham was a strong and impressive leader of Boise Basin's Republicans. His death aroused violent emotions.

79.
Ferdinand Patterson, who killed Pinkham, was equally impressive physically, but for many he was the incarnation of evil.

Ferd Patterson

1863

could try and hang a man without hearing a particle of evidence or knowing anything whatever about the case."

From the *World*'s point of view, vigilantes were nothing but "stranglers" who had created a reign of terror in which any person could be chased out of the Territory or killed without a trial or hearing. Vigilantes, like lynch mobs and others who took the law into their own hands, may have occasionally rid the world of scoundrels, but they also made mistakes and were guilty of murdering innocent men.

Ferd Patterson's trial, at the beginning of November, 1865, was reported nearly verbatim in the pages of the *World*.

Testimony of numerous eye-witnesses was vague or contradictory, and the jury was unable to determine who had fired first. The usual verdict of "not guilty" was rendered, since there was at least the possibility that Patterson had acted in self-defense. To Republicans it was an assassination, and the acquittal was achieved through the perjured testimony of Patterson's friends.

Pistols and Politics

The Pinkham-Patterson affair clearly showed that strong political feelings and firearms were an explosive mixture. A Democrat, writing in 1869, gave his party's view of what happened:

> Magnifying a purely personal affair, of so unfortunate a result, into a political cause of enmity, hundreds were induced to enter into an armed organization for the purpose, open and avowed, of breaking into the county jail, where Patterson was confined, and hanging him... the measures and precautions adopted by Sheriff Bowen and his Deputies were admirable. A *posse comitatus* of leading citizens of the county were summoned to defend the cause of law and order, to the number of nearly three hundred. The jail was put in a posture of defense, as perfect as the nature of the case permitted...

The author of the above, who used the pseudonym *Nemo*, listed the leading men on both sides. It was clearly a division along party lines. For the "defenders of law and order," all Democrats: "acting Sheriff A. O. Bowen, Under Sheriff J. J. Crutcher, Deputies Gorman, Donovan, Maloney and Tyson, and many special deputies, among the most active and efficient of whom were E. D. Holbrook, Delegate elect to Congress, John M. Murphy, County Auditor and Recorder, J. Marion More, George Ainslie and G. W. Thatcher."

Nemo's list of vigilante leaders, all Republican, included: Orlando Robbins, William McConnell, S. J. Henderson, Bailey Stepson, C. S. Kingsley and W. J. Gilkey. (Thomas Donaldson, a Republican appointee who came to Idaho a few years later, got to know many of the principals. He names Kingsley, a Methodist minister, as the organizer of the Idaho City vigilantes.) *Nemo* credits the wisdom and initiative of Under Sheriff James Crutcher and the good sense of Orlando "Rube" Robbins of the other side with averting a shootout between the nearly 300 men in each party. There could have been many deaths and a complete breakdown of law and order in the county. Fortunately, the vigilantes dispersed.

After his acquittal, Ferd Patterson left Idaho. Six months later he was shot to death while sitting in a barber chair in Walla Walla. Most old-timers were sure that he had been trailed there and killed by a vigilante assassin to avenge the death of Sumner Pinkham.

Differences among the Basin's Democrats were no less bitter than those with the Republicans. June, 1870, saw two gunfights that resulted in three deaths. Both involved well-known men in their communities. On June 18, former delegate to Congress E. D. Holbrook and Charles Douglass shot it out in front of Holbrook's Idaho City law office. Both men fired several times, but only Holbrook was hit. He died a few hours later. Douglass was tried and acquitted on grounds of self-defense. "The respectable element in the territory considered that Holbrook had been

80.
James J. Crutcher, Under Sheriff, helped defend the county jail against vigilantes in 1865.

81.
John Gorman, Deputy Sheriff, also defended Ferd Patterson against the mob.

82.
E. D. Holbrook, former Territorial Delegate in Congress, died in a shootout at Idaho City.

83.
Charles Douglass, who shot Holbrook, had to leave the country in a hurry.

84.
James A. Abbott killed his own brother as well as his enemy at Placerville.

assassinated," according to Thomas Donaldson, "and when tidings of the fatality reached Boise there was talk of a vigilance committee being organized. On all sides could be heard, "Charley got the drop on him."

Donaldson says that Douglass would have been lynched had he not left the Territory immediately. He was probably wise to run, since southern Idaho vigilantes had already taken care of several men.

The *Idaho World* called the gunfight that took place at Placerville June 25, 1870 "one of the most terrible tragedies that we have ever been called upon to chronicle." James A. Abbott, a farmer with a wife and five children, rode into town with his brother William and a hired hand named Curlen. They encountered a young Granite Creek miner named David H. Hannor on the plaza. (Bitter feeling had existed between Abbott and Hannor since Abbott had used "some rough language" at the Democratic county convention in April in opposition to Hannor's nomination as School Superintendent.)

After a brief exchange of words between the Abbotts and Hannor, the latter stepped forward, drawing his revolver as he did so. William Abbott, who was standing behind Hannor, shot him in the back of the head. James Abbott shot him in the forhead. Hannor died almost instantly, but one of James Abbott's bullets missed the mark and struck his brother in the abdomen. Curlen drew his weapon also, but did not fire.

William Abbott died later that evening and James Abbott was placed in jail and charged with murder. His first trial resulted in a hung jury, but at the second he was acquitted. As always, when both parties were armed, it was "self defense."

85

86

85.
Idaho City's Masonic Hall, built in 1865, is the oldest in the West still in use. It has changed little in the last 75 years.

86.
Idaho City Odd Fellows had this view of the town from their historic hall on East Hill.

87.
Bands serenaded the town from the balcony of the Idaho City Masonic Hall on many occasions in early days. Its style is Greek Revival. The bell tower no longer stands.

Afterword

88

89

By 1890 the small towns of Boise Basin were quiet and stable communities. Descendents of pioneers of the Sixties had intermarried until just about everybody was related in one way or another. Idaho City, Placerville, Centerville, Pioneerville, Granite Creek and Quartzburg were small enough places that you could call nearly everyone you met by name.

The names were familiar ones: Ainslie, Barry, Church, Emery, Garrecht, Gorman, Jones, Kempner, Kennaly, Kingsley, Lippincott, Luney, McClintock, Mantz, Silsby, Zipf. Most of these had been well-known in Idaho City for a quarter century. Chris Meffert still ran his Centerville hotel and saloon and the Coughanours were Quartzburg's pioneer family. Ben Willson still was the king-pin at Pioneerville. Placerville names known to everybody were Cathcart, Davidson, Donovan, Kohny, McDevitt, McKay, Myer, Rogan, Spencer, Stickel and Vesey.

Some of the old settlements had all but disappeared by 1890. Boston, located near the site of the discovery that got the Basin's gold rush started in 1862, called forth these nostalgic words in 1879:

> To stand at the head of Main street and gaze down as far as the silvery waters of "Old Grimes" and realize that the cruel hand of time is rapidly driving our beautiful "Hub" into oblivion is sad indeed. Population reduced to just a quorum for a solo game. Now and then days of yore flit to mind and dispel all thought of our present surroundings — days when even nature seemed to wear a gayer, brighter dress. Knock-down, drag-out, bite-and-gouge days, happy days that we shall know no more forever.

Large-scale hydraulic mining was eating up the sites of towns like Boston. In a few years, after gold dredges had been introduced into Basin streams, there was no longer a trace of many of the old camps. Although the excitement of the early gold rush was past by 1890, there were still millions of dollars worth of gold waiting to be extracted. The story of the Basin and its people after 1890 will be told in a companion volume to this one.

88 and 89.
Mr. and Mrs. Chris Meffert ran a Placerville hotel and saloon for more than 30 years. He was a native of Hungary.

90.
Prominent men of Boise Basin, 1864. E. D. Holbrook, far right, back row, and his friend, J. Marion More, seated in front of him, both died in gunfights. Others in the picture are, back row: Ben White, Lar Lindsay, N. B. Wood; front row, Sank Owens, John Weller, Green White.

91.
Dryden McClintock ran Idaho City's leading livery stable for a generation. He was one of the Basin's most popular pioneers.

92.
After J. Marion More was killed a friend wrote "No citizen of Boise County has ever been called from earth more universally known, beloved, esteemed and regretted."

90

91

92

93.
David Coughanour and his family posed for the photographer in front of their substantial Quartzburg house. Their Chinese cook can be seen near the center of the picture.

94.
These Quartzburg folks were all dressed up to celebrate July 4, 1890 — the day after Idaho was admitted to the Union as the 43rd state.

Acknowledgements

This book would not have been written without the encouragement and support of the Idaho City Historical Foundation. To all of my friends in Idaho City, but particularly to Byron Johnson, John Brogan and Ken Smith, a special thank you.

I am again indebted to the helpful and talented people at the Idaho State Historical Library: Judith Austin, Gary Gettis, Guila Ford, Elizabeth Jacox, Larry Jones, Merle Wells and Marjorie Williams. All of the illustrations used in this book are from the collections of the Idaho City Historical Foundation and the Idaho State Historical Society.

Some of the material used here appeared first in my weekly column in the *Idaho Statesman*, and is reprinted by permission.

A great number of sources were used in researching *Basin of Gold*, but early issues of the *Idaho World* and the *Idaho Tri-weekly Statesman* were especially valuable for capturing the flavor of times, places and people. Quotations from Thomas Donaldson's *Idaho of Yesterday* were used by permission of Caxton Printers, Ltd.

My thanks to Historic Boise, Incorporated, and its Board of Directors for agreeing to co-sponsor publication of *Basin of Gold*. Robert Aldridge, Robert Auth, Duane Garrett, Barbara Hansen, Kay Hardy, Linda Hildeman, Ernest Lombard, Susan Stacy and Jean Wilson have been helpful and supportive.

Finally, to my worthy partner in this and all other endeavors, my wife, Novella Dee, my love and special gratitude.

Arthur A. Hart